GROWING IN CHRIST

GROWING IN CHRIST

J. I. Packer

Published Originally Under The Title
I Want to Be a Christian

CROSSWAY BOOKS • WHEATON, ILLINOIS
A DIVISION OF GOOD NEWS PUBLISHERS

To
Jim, Tom,
and Elisabeth
who by what they
are even more than
by what they say
share the strength they
have been given

Contents

PART FOUR
DESIGN FOR LIFE:
THE TEN COMMANDMENTS

Introduction

The motive that led me to write *Growing in Christ* was to provide a resource book for study groups, and also a do-it-yourself study course for adults who have no access to such a group. From that standpoint, this is a companion piece to my book, *Knowing God*, which has been used widely for group discussion. It offers a series of quick, brief outlines—"sprints" if you will—with questions and Bible passages for further study, covering the contents of the three formulae which have always been central in Christian teaching—the Creed, the Lord's Prayer, and the Ten Commandments, plus Christian baptism. These three formulae deal with the Christian's convictions, communion with God, and code of conduct respectively; baptism speaks of God's covenant, Christian conversion and commitment, and church life. Baptism is put in its logical place as the second part of the book, straight after our study of the faith into which Christians are baptized, and leading on to reflections on prayer and obedience as expressions of the life of discipleship.

My hope is that the book may have a use in all churches where the historic faith is held, and to this end I have confined my material to matters which C. S. Lewis called (borrowing from Richard Baxter) "mere Christianity." I have, therefore, sought to focus on the essentials of the faith, except for three inescapable references to historical misunderstandings of the Creed and the gospel by the Roman Catholic Church (misunderstandings which many Roman Catholic theologians now labor to transcend).

The "sprints," which are written in as compressed and suggestive a way as I can manage, are only pipe-openers, to start you talking and thinking; for anything like a full treatment of each topic, readers must go on to the questions and the Bible study.

Many Christians today are uncomfortable with the word "catechism," but they need not be. *Catechism* simply comes from a Greek word meaning "make to hear" and so "instruct." From this word comes the English words of *catechism* (the form of instruction), *catechumen* (the person under instruction), *catechumenate* (the organized set-up for giving instruction), and *catechize* (a verb which originally meant "instruct," though today it refers especially to a question-and-answer method of teaching). In Acts 8 we read how Philip instructed the Ethiopian eunuch; catechizing is just that process institutionalized.

Christianity is not instinctive to anyone, nor is it picked up casually without effort. It is a faith that has to be learned, and therefore taught, and so some sort of systematic instruction (*catechumenate*) is an essential part of a church's life.

In the first Christian centuries there was a steady stream of adult converts and enquirers, and catechetical instruction took the form of lectures, given at their level. The Reformers' strategy for revitalizing a Christendom that was ignorant of Christianity led them, however, to concentrate on systematic instruction for children. During a century and a half following Luther's pioneer *Little Catechism* of 1529, literally hundreds of catechisms were produced, mostly though not exclusively for the young. Some of these were official church documents, others the private compositions of individual clergymen. The English Prayer Book catechism, the Heidelberg Catechism, and the Westminster Shorter Catechism are among the best known. Probably most Protestants today associate catechisms and catechizing exclusively with nurturing children, and would not think of presentations like C. S. Lewis's *Mere Christianity*, or Billy Graham's *Peace with God*, or John Stott's *Basic Christianity*, or G. K. Chesterton's *Orthodoxy*, as catechetical, because they are written for adults. But inasmuch as they are intended to instruct outsiders and establish insiders in fundamentals of the faith, catechetical is their proper description.

One great need today is a renewal of systematic Christian instruction—catechetical teaching—for adults. It need not be called that, nor need it take the form of rigid drilling in preset formulae, which is how old-time Protestants taught their children; but somehow or other, opportunities must be given for folk in and just outside the churches to examine Christian essentials, because there are so many for whom this is a prime need. Preaching often does not help them, for preaching ordinarily assumes in both speaker and hearers confident certainty about the fundamentals of the faith, and where this is lacking, sermons are felt to be remote and even irritating because of what appear as their unexamined assumptions. But the proper place for examining, challenging, and testing the intellectual ABCs of Christianity is not the pulpit, but rather the systematic instruction given in catechetical teaching—at least, so Christian history suggests.

Modern educational theory sets great store by individual exploration, personal discovery, and group discussion, and there is no reason why today's adult instruction should not take this form—indeed, it will be best if it does, provided we remember that Christianity has a given content and continuity, and is not an "x," an undefined quantity, to be re-invented through discussion in each new generation! C. H. Spurgeon's wicked story of the Irishman who, asked how he got on at the meeting of a small separatist church said, "Oh, it was lovely; none of us knew anything, and we all taught each other," has a message for us here. One has known professedly Christian groups professedly studying Christian fundamentals on which this story would make a very apt comment. Guided study groups on Christian Basics, however, such as some churches known to me run year after year, constitute a genuine and much-needed renewal of the catechumenate—that is, the systematic teaching of Christian essentials—and I do not expect ever to find a church that would not benefit from their introduction.

It is my hope that this book may be used in some small way to help many come to a deeper understanding of the essentials of the Christian Faith, and, as the title indicates, to grow in our Lord and Savior, Jesus Christ.

J. I. PACKER

Part One

Affirming the Essentials:

The Apostles' Creed

The Apostles' Creed

I believe in God the Father almighty,
maker of heaven and earth;
and in Jesus Christ
his only Son our Lord,
who was conceived by the Holy Spirit,
born of the Virgin Mary,
suffered under Pontius Pilate,
was crucified, dead, and buried:
he descended into hell;
the third day he rose again from the dead;
he ascended into heaven,
and sitteth on the right hand of God the Father
  almighty;
from thence he shall come to judge the quick and
  the dead.
I believe in the Holy Spirit;
the holy catholic church;
the communion of saints;
the forgiveness of sins;
the resurrection of the body,
and the life everlasting.

Preface

If you are going to travel cross-country on foot, you need a map. Now there are different kinds of maps. One sort is the large-scale relief map, which marks all the paths, bogs, crags, and so on in detail. Since the walker needs the fullest information about his chosen route, he must have a map of that sort. But for choosing between the various ways he might go, he could well learn more, and more quickly, from a small-scale map which left out the detailed geography and just showed him the roads and trails leading most directly from one place to another. Well-prepared walkers have maps of both kinds.

If life is a journey, then the million-word-long Holy Bible is the large-scale map with everything in it, and the hundred-word Apostles' Creed (so called, not because apostles wrote it—despite later legend, they didn't—but because it teaches apostolic doctrine) is the simplified road map, ignoring much but enabling you to see at a glance the main points of Christian belief. "Creed" means "belief"; many Christians of former days used to call this Creed "the Belief," and in the second century, when it first appeared, almost as we have it now, it was called the Rule of Faith.

When folk enquire into Christianity, their advisers naturally want to get them studying the Bible and to lead them into personal trust in the living Christ as soon as they can; and rightly so. But as means to both ends, it helps to take them through the Creed, as both a preliminary orientation to the Bible and a preliminary analysis of the convictions on which faith in Christ must rest.

Those convictions are trinitarian. The Creed tells us of Father, Son, and Holy Spirit, so that having found out about them we might find them experientially. What do we learn from the Creed, as we study it? The answer has been summarized beautifully as follows:

"First, I learn to believe in God the Father, who hath made me, and all the world.

"Secondly, in God the Son who hath redeemed me, and all mankind.

"Thirdly, in God the Holy Ghost, who sanctifieth me, and all the elect people of God."[1]

When one has learned this much, one is not far from God's kingdom.

The purpose of knowledge is that we might apply it to life. This is nowhere truer than in Christianity, where true knowledge (knowledge of the true God) is precisely knowledge about God—applied. And knowledge about God, for application, is what is offered here, in the studies that follow.

Note:

[1] *The Prayer Book Catechism.*

1

I Believe in God

When people are asked what they believe in, they give, not merely different answers, but different sorts of answers. Someone might say, "I believe in UFOs"—that means, I think UFOs are real. "I believe in democracy"—that means, I think democratic principles are just and beneficial. But what does it mean when Christian congregations stand and say: "I believe in God"? Far more than when the object of belief is UFOs or democracy.

I can believe in UFOs without ever looking for one, and in democracy without ever voting. In cases like these, belief is a matter of the intellect only. But the Creed's opening words, "I believe in God," render a Greek phrase coined by the writers of the New Testament, meaning literally: "I *am believing into* God." That is to say, over and above believing certain truths *about* God, I am living in a relation of commitment *to* God in trust and union. When I say "I believe in God," I am professing my conviction that God has invited me to this commitment, and declaring that I have accepted his invitation.

Faith

The word "faith," which is English for a Greek noun (*pistis*) formed from the verb in the phrase "believe into" (*pisteuo*), gets the idea of trustful commitment and reliance better than "belief" does. Whereas "belief" suggests bare opinion, "faith," whether in a car, a patent medicine, a protégé, a doctor, a marriage partner, or what have you, is a matter of treating the person or thing as trustworthy and committing yourself accordingly. The same is true of faith in God, and in a more far-reaching way.

It is the offer and demand of the object that determines in each case what a faith-commitment involves. Thus, I show faith in my car by relying on it to get me places, and in my doctor by submitting to his treatment. And I show faith in God by bowing to his claim to rule and manage me; by receiving Jesus Christ, his Son, as my own Lord and Savior; and by relying on his promise to bless me here and hereafter. This is the meaning of response to the offer and demand of the God of the Creed.

Sometimes faith is equated with that awareness of "one above" (or "beyond," or "at the heart of things") which from time to time, through the impact of nature, conscience, great art, being in love, or whatever, touches the hearts of the hardest-boiled. (Whether they take it seriously is another question, but it comes to all—God sees to that.) But Christian faith only begins when we attend to God's self-disclosure in Christ and in Scripture, where we meet him as the Creator who "commands all men everywhere to repent" and to "believe in the name of his Son Jesus Christ . . . as he has commanded us" (Acts 17:30; 1 John 3:23; cf. John 6:28 ff.). Christian faith means hearing, noting, and doing what God says.

Doubt

I write as if God's revelation in the Bible has self-evident truth and authority, and I think that in the last analysis it has; but I know, as you do, that uncriticized preconceptions and prejudices create problems for us all, and many have deep doubts and perplexities about elements of the biblical message. How do these doubts relate to faith?

Well, what is doubt? It is a state of divided mind—"double-mindedness" is James' concept (James 1:6-8)—and it is found both *within* faith and *without* it. In the former case, it is faith infected, sick, and out of sorts; in the latter, it belongs to a struggle either toward faith or away from a God felt to be invading and making claims one does not want to meet. In C. S. Lewis' spiritual autobiography, *Surprised by Joy*, you can observe both these motivations successively.

In our doubts, we think we are honest, and certainly try to be; but perfect honesty is beyond us in this world, and an unacknowledged unwillingness to take God's word about things, whether from deference to supposed scholarship or fear of ridicule or of deep involvement or from some other motive, often underlies a person's doubt about this or that item of faith. Repeatedly this becomes clear in retrospect, though we could not see it at the time.

How can one help doubters? First, by *explaining* the problem area (for doubts often arise from misunderstanding); second, by *exhibiting* the reasonableness of Christian belief at that point, and the grounds for embracing it (for Christian beliefs, though above reason, are not against it); third, by *exploring* what prompts the doubts (for doubts are never rationally compelling, and hesitations about Christianity usually have more to do with likes and dislikes, hurt feelings, and social, intellectual, and cultural snobbery than the doubters are aware).

Personal

In worship, the Creed is said in unison, but the opening words are "I believe"—not "we": each worshiper speaks for himself. Thus he proclaims his philosophy of life, and at the same time testifies to his happiness: he has come into the hands of the Christian God where he is glad to be, and when he says "I believe," it is an act of praise and thanksgiving on his part. It is in truth a great thing to be able to say the Creed.

Further Bible Study

Faith in action:
- Romans 4
- Hebrews 11
- Mark 5:25-34

Questions for Thought and Discussion

- What is the essential meaning of "faith" (Greek pistis)?
- What is the importance of the word "I" in the Creed's opening phrase?

- What doubts about Christianity have you had to deal with in yourself and others?
- How can the approach outlined in this chapter help address doubts and questions we may have?

2

The God I Believe In

What should it mean when we stand in church and say, "I believe in God"? Are we at this point just allying ourselves with Jews, Moslems, Hindus, and others against atheism, and declaring that there is some God as distinct from none? No; we are doing far more than this. We are professing faith in the God of the Creed itself, the Christian God, the God of the Bible—the Sovereign Creator whose "Christian name," as Karl Barth put it, is Father, Son, and Holy Spirit. If this is not the God in whom we believe, we have no business saying the Creed at all.

Idols

We must be clear here. Today's idea is that the great divide is between those who say "I believe in God" in some sense, and those who cannot say it in any sense. Atheism is seen as an enemy, paganism is not, and it is assumed that the difference between one faith and another is quite secondary. But in the Bible the great divide is between those who believe in the Christian God and those who serve idols—"gods," that is, whose images, whether metal or mental, do not square with the self-disclosure of the Creator. One wishes that some who recite "I believe in God" in church each Sunday would see that what they actually mean is "I do *not* believe in God—not this God, anyhow!"

His Name

The Bible tells us that God has revealed himself, establishing his identity, so to speak, by telling us his "name." This "name" appears in three connections.

First, God gave his "proper name," JEHOVAH (or Yahweh, as modern scholars prefer), to Moses at the burning bush (Exodus 3:13ff.; see also 6:3). The name means "I am who I am," or "I will be what I will be" (RSV, text and margin). It declares God's almightiness: he cannot be hindered from being what he is, and doing what he wills. Well did the AV translators render this name as "the LORD." The Creed echoes this emphasis when it speaks of God the Father *almighty*.

Second, God "proclaimed the name of the LORD" to Moses by delineating his moral character—"a God merciful and gracious, slow to anger, and abounding in steadfast love and faithfulness, keeping steadfast love for thousands, forgiving iniquity . . . but who will by no means clear the guilty . . . " (Exodus 34:5-7). This "name"—you could call it a revealed description—discloses both God's *nature* and his *role*. It is a declaration whose echoes reverberate throughout the Bible (see Exodus 20:5 ff.; Numbers 14:18; 2 Chronicles 30:9; Nehemiah 1:5; 9:17, 32; Psalm 86:5, 15; 103:8-18; 111:4-9; 112:4; 116:5; 145:8 ff., 17, 20; Joel 2:13; Jonah 4:2; Romans 2:2-6), and all God's acts which Scripture records confirm and illustrate its truth. It is noteworthy that when John focuses the two sides of God's character by saying that he is both *light* and *love* (1 John 1:5; 4:8)—not love without righteousness and purity, nor rectitude without kindness and compassion, but holy love, and loving holiness, and each quality to the highest degree—he offers each statement as summarizing what we learn from Jesus about God.

Three in One

Third, the Son of God told his disciples to baptize "in the name of the Father and of the Son and of the Holy Spirit" (Matthew 28:19). "Name," note, not "names": the three persons together constitute the one God. Here we face the most dizzying and unfathomable truth of all, the truth of the Trinity, to which the three paragraphs of the Creed (" the Father . . . his only Son . . . the Holy Spirit") also bear witness.

What should we make of it? In itself, the divine tri-unity is a mystery, a transcendent fact which passes our understanding. (The same is true of such realities as God's eternity, infinity, omniscience, and providential control of our free actions; indeed, all truths about God exceed our comprehension, more or less.) How the one eternal God is eternally both singular and plural, how Father, Son, and Spirit are personally distinct yet essentially one (so that tritheism, belief in three gods who are not one, and Unitarianism, belief in one God who is not three, are both wrong), is more than we can know, and any attempt to "explain" it—to dispel the mystery by reasoning, as distinct from confessing it from Scripture—is bound to falsify it. Here, as elsewhere, our God is too big for his creatures' little minds.

Yet the historical foundation-facts of Christian faith—a man who was God, praying to his Father and promising that he and his father would send "another Comforter" to continue his divine ministry—and equally the universally experienced facts of Christian devotion—worshipping God the Father above you and knowing the fellowship of God the Son beside you, both through the prompting of God the Holy Spirit within you—point inescapably to God's essential three-in-oneness. So does the cooperative activity of the Three in saving us—the Father planning, the Son procuring, and the Spirit applying redemption. Many Scriptures witness to this: see, for instance, Romans 8:1-17; 2 Corinthians 13:14; Ephesians 1:3-14; 2 Thessalonians 2:13 ff.; 1 Peter 1:2. When the gospel of Christ is analyzed, the truth of the Trinity proves to be its foundation and framework.

It was only through the work of grace which centers on the Incarnation that the one God was seen to be plural. No wonder, then, if those who do not believe in the work of grace doubt the truth of the Trinity too.

But this is the God of the Creed. Is this, now, the God whom we worship? Or have we too fallen victims to idolatry?

Further Bible Study

God revealed:
1 John 1:1-18

Questions for Thought and Discussion

- What does it mean to say: "In the Bible the great divide is between those who believe in the Christian God and those who serve idols"? Do you agree or disagree? Why?
- What is the basic meaning of God's name JEHOVAH? What does it tell us about him?
- Why did Christ direct his disciples to baptize "in the name (singular) of the Father and of the Son and of the Holy Spirit"?

3

The Father Almighty

In any church where saying the Creed is part of the worship service it is likely that God's fatherhood will have been celebrated in song ("Glory be to the Father . . . ") before the Creed is said, for it is a theme which with a sure instinct hymn writers have always highlighted. But how should we understand it?

Creation

Clearly, when the Creed speaks of "God the Father almighty, maker of heaven and earth," it has in immediate view the fact that we and all things besides depend on God as Creator for our existence, every moment. Now to call creatorship fatherhood is not unscriptural: it echoes both the Old Testament—Malachi 2:10, "Have we not all one father? Has not one God created us?" and the New Testament—Acts 17:28, where Paul preaching at Athens quotes with approval a Greek poet's statement: *we are his offspring.* Nonetheless, both these quotations come from passages threatening divine judgment, and Paul's evangelistic sermon at Athens makes it very clear that though the offspring relationship implies an obligation to seek, worship, and obey God, and makes one answerable to him at the end of the day, it does not imply his favor and acceptance where repentance for past sins and faith in Christ are lacking (see the whole speech, verses 22-31).

Some who stress the universal fatherhood of God treat it as implying that all men are and always will be in a state of salvation, but that is not the biblical view. Paul speaks of persons to whom "the word of the cross is folly" as "perishing" (1 Corinthians 1:18), and warns the "impenitent" that "you are storing up wrath for yourself on the day of wrath" (Romans 2:5), however much they are God's offspring.

Father and Son

In fact, when the New Testament speaks of God's fatherhood it is not with reference to creation, but in two further connections. The first is *the inner life of the Godhead*. Within the eternal Trinity is a family relation of Father and Son. On earth, the Son called the One whom he served "my Father" and prayed to him as Abba—the Aramaic equivalent of a respectful Dad.

What this relationship meant Jesus himself declared. On the one hand, the Son loves the Father (John 14:31) and always does what pleases the Father (8:29). He takes no initiatives, depending instead every moment on the Father for a lead (5:19ff., 30), but he is tenacity itself in cleaving to the Father's known will. "My Father . . . not as I will, but as thou wilt . . . thy will be done" (Matthew 26:39, 42). "Shall I not drink the cup which the Father has given me?" (John 18:11).

On the other hand, the Father loves the Son (John 3:35; 5:20) and makes him great by giving him glory and great things to do (5:20-30; 10:17ff.; 17:23-26). Giving life and executing judgment are twin tasks which have been wholly committed to him, "that all may honor the Son" (5:23).

God's loving fatherhood of his eternal Son is both the archetype of his gracious relationship with his own redeemed people and the model from which derives the parenthood that God has created in human families. Paul spoke of "the God and Father of our Lord Jesus Christ" as "the Father, from whom every family in heaven and on earth is named" (Ephesians 1:3; 3:14ff.). Human families, by their very constitution, reflect the Father-Son relationship in heaven, and parent-child relationships should express a love that corresponds to the mutual love of Father and Son in the Godhead.

Adoption

The second connection in which the New Testament speaks of God as Father has to do with *the believing sinner's adoption* into the life of God's family. This is a supernatural gift of grace, linked with justification and new birth, given freely by God and received humbly by faith in Jesus Christ as Savior and Lord. "To all who received him [Jesus], who believed in his name, he gave power to become children of God; who were born . . . of God . . ." (John 1:12ff.). The message Jesus sent to his disciples on rising from the dead was: "I am ascending to my Father and your Father, to my God and your God" (John 20:17). As disciples, they belonged to the family; indeed, in that very sentence Jesus called them "my brethren." All whom he has saved are his brothers.

When the Christian says the first clause of the Creed, he will put all this together and confess his Creator as both the Father of his Savior and his own Father through Christ—a Father who now loves him no less than he loves his only begotten Son. That is a marvelous confession to be able to make.

Almighty

And God the Father is "almighty"—which means that he can and will do all that he intends. What does he intend for his sons? Answer: that they should share all that their elder Brother enjoys now. Believers are "heirs of God, and fellow heirs with Christ, provided we suffer with him in order that we may also be glorified with him" (Romans 8:17). Suffer we shall, but we shall not miss the glory: the Father almighty will see to that. Praise his name.

Further Bible Study

On our adoption in Christ:
- Ephesians 1:3-14
- Galatians 4:1-7

Questions for Thought and Discussion

- What does the statement "we are his offspring" say about God's fatherhood? What does it leave out?
- How is God's fatherhood seen within the Trinity?
- Why can Jesus call Christians his "brethren"?

4

Almighty

The Creed declares faith in God the Father *almighty*. Does the adjective matter? Yes, a great deal. It points to the basic Bible fact that God is the Lord, the King, the omnipotent one who reigns over his world. Note the ecstatic joy with which God's sovereign rule is proclaimed and praised in (for instance) Psalm 93, 96, 97, 99:1-5, and 103. Men treat God's sovereignty as a theme for controversy, but in Scripture it is matter for worship.

We need to realize that you cannot rightly understand God's ways at any point till you see them in the light of his sovereignty. That, no doubt, is why the Creed takes the first opportunity of announcing it. But, though the believing heart warms to it, it is not an easy truth for our minds to grasp, and a number of questions arise.

What God Cannot Do

First, does omnipotence mean that God can do literally anything? No, that is not the meaning. There are many things God cannot do. He cannot do what is self-contradictory or nonsensical, like squaring the circle. Nor (and this is vital) can he act out of character. God has a perfect moral character, and it is not in him to deny it. He cannot be capricious, unloving, random, unjust, or inconsistent. Just as he cannot pardon sin without atonement, because that would not

31

be right, so he cannot fail to be "faithful and just" in forgiving sins that are confessed in faith, and in keeping all the other promises he has made, for failure here would not be right either. Moral instability, vacillation, and unreliability are marks of weakness, not of strength: but God's omnipotence is supreme strength, making it impossible that he should lapse into imperfections of this sort.

The positive way to say this is that though there are things which a holy, rational God is incapable of intending, all that he intends to do he actually does. "Whatever the Lord pleases he does" (Psalm 135:6). As, when he planned to make the world, "he spoke and it came to be" (Psalm 33:9; see Genesis 1), so with each other thing that he wills. With men, "there's many a slip 'twixt cup and lip," but not with him.

Human Free Will

Second, is not God's power to fulfill his purposes limited by the free will of man? No. Man's power of spontaneous and responsible choice is a created thing, an aspect of the mystery of created human nature, and God's power to fulfill his purposes is not limited by anything that he has made. Just as he works out his will through the functioning of the physical order, so he works out his will through the functioning of our psychological makeup. In no case is the integrity of the created thing affected, and it is always possible (apart from some miracles) to "explain" what has happened without reference to the rule of God. But in every case God orders the things that come to pass.

So, therefore, without violating the nature of created realities, or reducing man's activity to robot level, God still "accomplishes all things according to the counsel of his will" (Ephesians 1:11).

But surely in that case what we think of as our free will is illusory and unreal? That depends on what you mean. It is certainly illusory to think that our wills are only free if they operate apart from God. But free will in the sense of "free agency," as theologians have defined it—that is, the power of spontaneous, self-determining choice referred to above—is real. As a fact of creation, an aspect of our humanness, it exists, as all created things do, in God. How God sustains it and overrules it without overriding it is his secret; but that he does so is certain, both from our conscious experience

32

of making decisions and acting "of our own free will," and also from Scripture's sobering insistence that we are answerable to God for our actions, just because in the moral sense they really are ours.

Evil is Mastered

Third, does not the existence of evil—moral badness, useless pain, and waste of good—suggest that God the Father is not almighty after all?—for surely he would remove these things if he could? Yes, he would, and he is doing so! Through Christ, bad folk like you and me are already being made good; new pain- and disease-free bodies are on the way, and a reconstructed cosmos with them; and Paul assures us that "the sufferings of this present time are not worth comparing with the glory that is to be revealed to us" (Romans 8:18; cf. 19-23). If God moves more slowly than we wish in clearing evil out of his world and introducing the new order, that, we may be sure, is in order to widen his gracious purpose and include in it more victims of the world's evil than otherwise he could have done. (Study 2 Peter 3:3-10, especially verse 8ff.)

Good News

The truth of God's almightiness in creation, providence, and grace is the basis of all our trust, peace, and joy in God, and the safeguard of all our hopes of answered prayer, present protection, and final salvation. It means that neither fate, nor the stars, nor blind chance, nor man's folly, nor Satan's malice controls this world; instead, a morally perfect God runs it, and none can dethrone him or thwart his purposes of love. And if I am Christ's, then—

A sovereign protector I have,
Unseen, yet forever at hand,
Unchangeably faithful to save,
Almighty to rule and command . . .
If thou art my Shield and my Sun
The night is no darkness to me,
And, fast as my moments roll on,
They bring me but nearer to thee.

Good news? Yes, the best ever.

Further Bible Study

God the overruler:
- Genesis 50:15-26
- Psalm 93
- Acts 4:23-31

Questions for Thought and Discussion

- What does "almighty" mean? Why is it important to believe that God is almighty?
- In what sense, if any, is it true to say that there are some things which even omnipotence cannot do?
- Is God's power limited by man's free will? Why or why not?

5

Maker of Heaven
and Earth

In the beginning God created the heavens and the earth"; so begins the Bible. ("Heavens and earth" is Bible language for "everything that is.")

It is arguable how much (or how little) Genesis 1 and 2 tell us about the *method* of creation—whether, for instance, they do or do not rule out the idea of physical organisms evolving through epochs of thousands of years. What is clear, however, is that their main aim is to tell us not how the world was made, but who made it.

Introducing the Artist

The solution-chapter in one of Dorothy Sayers' detective stories is called "When You Know How You Know Who." Genesis 1 and 2, however, tell us *who* without giving many answers about *how*. Some today may think this a defect; but in the long perspective of history our present-day "scientific" preoccupation with *how* rather than *who* looks very odd in itself. Rather than criticize these chapters for not feeding our secular interest, we should take from them needed rebuke of our perverse passion for knowing Nature without regard for what matters most; namely, knowing Nature's Creator.

The message of these two chapters is this: "You have seen the sea? the sky? sun, moon and stars? You have watched the birds and the fish? You have observed the landscape, the vegetation, the animals, the insects, all the big things and little things together? You have marveled at the wonderful complexity of human beings, with all their powers and skills, and the deep feelings of fascination, attraction, and affection that men and women arouse in each other? Fantastic, isn't it? Well now, meet the one who is behind it all!" As if to say: now that you have enjoyed these works of art, you must shake hands with the artist; since you were thrilled by the music, we will introduce you to the composer. It was to show us the Creator rather than the creation, and to teach us knowledge of God rather than physical science, that Genesis 1 and 2, along with such celebrations of creation as Psalm 104 and Job 38-41, were written.

In creating, God was craftsman and more. Craftsmen shape existing material, and are limited by it, but no material existed at all till God said "Let there be . . . " To make this point theologians speak of creation "out of nothing," meaning not that nothing was a sort of a something(!) but that God in creating was absolutely free and unrestricted, and that nothing determined or shaped what he brought into being save his own idea of what he would like.

Creator and Creature

The Creator-creature distinction is basic to the Bible view of God's lordship in providence and grace, and indeed to all true thought about God and man. That is why it is in the Creed. Its importance is at least threefold.

First, *it stops misunderstanding of God.* God made us in his image, but we tend to think of him in ours! ("Man made God in his own image" was a crack by Voltaire, rather too true to be good.) But the Creator-creature distinction reminds us that God does not depend on us as we depend on him, nor does he exist by our will and for our pleasure, nor may we think of his personal life as being just like ours. As creatures we are limited; we cannot know everything at once, nor be present everywhere, nor do all we should like to do, nor continue unchanged through the years. But the Creator is not limited in these ways. Therefore we find him *incomprehensible*—by which I mean, not *making no sense,* but *exceeding our grasp.* We can no more take his measure than our dogs and cats can take our measure. When Luther told Erasmus that his thoughts of God were *too human*, he was uprooting in principle all the rationalistic religion that has ever infected the church—and rightly too! We must learn to be self-critical in our thinking about God.

Second, *this distinction stops misunderstanding of the world*. The world exists in its present stable state by the will and power of its Maker. Since it is his world, we are not its owners, free to do as we like with it, but its stewards, answerable to him for the way we handle its resources. And since it is his world, we must not depreciate it. Much religion has built on the idea that the material order—reality as experienced through the body, along with the body that experiences it—is evil, and therefore to be refused and ignored as far as possible. This view, which dehumanizes its devotees, has sometimes called itself Christian, but it is really as un-Christian as can be. For matter, being made by God, was and is *good* in his eyes (Genesis 1:31), and so should be so in ours (1 Timothy 4:4). We serve God by using and enjoying temporal things gratefully, with a sense of their value to him, their Maker, and of his generosity in giving them to us. It is an ungodly and, indeed, inhuman super-spirituality which seeks to serve the Creator by depreciating any part of his creation.

Third, *this distinction stops misunderstanding of ourselves*. As man is not his own maker, so he may not think of himself as his own master. "God made me for himself, to serve him here." God's claim upon us is the first fact of life that we must face, and we need a healthy sense of our creaturehood to keep us facing it.

Further Bible Study

God the Creator:
- Genesis 1, 2
- Isaiah 45:9-25

Questions for Thought and Discussion

- What is the significance of God's words "Let there be . . . "?
- What does the "Creator-creature distinction" have to do with God making man in his own image?
- Why can we say with confidence that the material order is not evil?

6

And in Jesus Christ

I believe in God the Father . . . and in Jesus Christ his only Son our Lord." So the Creed declares. When it called God "maker of heaven and earth," it parted company with Hinduism and Eastern faiths generally; now, by calling Jesus Christ God's only Son, it parts company with Judaism and Islam and stands quite alone. This claim for Jesus is both the touchstone of Christianity and the ingredient that makes it unique. As the whole New Testament was written to make and justify the claim, we should not be surprised when we find the Creed stating it with fuller detail than it states anything else.

Christ and the Center

This claim is central to the layout of the Creed, for the long section on Jesus Christ stands between the two shorter sections on the Father and the Spirit. And it is central to the faith of the Creed, for we could not know about the Trinity, or salvation, or resurrection and life everlasting, apart from Jesus Christ. It was Jesus Christ, in his redemption of all God's people, who was the revealer of all these truths.

See how the Creed presents him.

Jesus (Greek for Joshua, meaning "God is Savior") is his proper name. It identifies him as a historical person, Mary's son from Nazareth in Galilee, a Jewish ex-carpenter who worked for three years as a rural rabbi and was put to death by the Roman authorities about A.D. 30. The four Gospels describe his ministry in some detail.

Christ (literally, "the anointed one") is not a surname, except in the old sense in which surnames like Smith, Taylor, Packer, or Clark declared a man's trade or profession. "Christ" is what Presbyterians would call an "office-title," identifying Jesus as God's appointed savior-king for whom the Jews had long been waiting. Since the Christ was expected to set up God's reign and be hailed as overlord throughout the world, to call Jesus *Christ* was to claim for him a decisive place in history and a universal dominion which all men everywhere must acknowledge. The first Christians did this quite self-consciously; one sees them doing it in the speeches recorded in Acts (see 2:22-36; 3:12-26; 5:29-32; 10:34-43; 13:26-41; etc.). "To this end Christ died and lived again, that he might be Lord both of the dead and of the living" (Romans 14:9). "At the name of Jesus every knee should bow" (Philippians 2:10).

Also, the title *Christ* expresses the claim that Jesus fulfilled all three ministries for which men were anointed in Old Testament times, being *prophet* (a messenger from God) and *priest* (one who mediates with God for us by sacrifice) as well as being *king*.

The glory of this conjunction of roles is only seen when we relate it to our actual needs. What do we sinners need for a right and good relationship with God? First, we are ignorant of him and need instruction—for no satisfying relationship is possible with a person about whom you know little or nothing. Second, we are estranged from him and need reconciliation—otherwise we shall end up unaccepted, unforgiven, and unblessed, strangers to his fatherly love and exiles from the inheritance which is in store for those who are his children. Third, we are weak, blind, and foolish when it comes to the business of living for God, and we need someone to guide, protect, and strengthen us—which is how the regal role was understood in Old Testament Israel. Now in the person and ministry of the one man, Jesus Christ, this threefold need is completely and perfectly met! Hallelujah!

Great Prophet of my God!
My tongue would bless thy name;
By thee the joyful news
Of our salvation came;
The joyful news of sins forgiven,
Of hell subdued, and peace with heaven.

Jesus, my great High Priest,
Offered his blood and died;
My guilty conscience seeks
No sacrifice beside;
His powerful blood did once atone,
And now it pleads before the throne.

My dear Almighty Lord,
My conqueror and my King,
Thy sceptre, and thy sword,
Thy reigning grace I sing.
Thine is the power; behold, I sit
In willing bonds before thy feet.

The Divine Lord

Jesus, who is the Christ (says the Creed), is God's *only Son.* This identifies Mary's boy as the second person of the eternal Trinity, the Word who was the Father's agent in making the world and sustaining it right up to the present (John 1:1-4; Colossians 1:13-20; Hebrews 1:1-3). Staggering? Yes, certainly, but this identification is the heart of Christianity. "The word of God became a human being and lived among us" (John 1:14, Phillips).

"Our Lord" follows straight from this. If Jesus is God the Son, our co-creator, and is also Christ, the anointed savior-king, now risen from death and reigning (sitting, as the Creed puts it, "on the right hand of God the Father almighty," in the place of authority and power), then he has a right to rule us, and we have no right to resist his claim. As he invaded space and time in Palestine nearly 2,000 years ago, so he invades our personal space and time today, with the same purpose of love that first brought him to earth. "Come, follow me" was his word then, and it is so still.

Is he, then, your Lord? For all who say the Creed, this question is inescapable; for how can you say "our Lord" in church till you have first said "my Lord" in your heart?

Further Bible Study

Jesus—God and man:
• Hebrews 1:1-3:6

Questions for Thought and Discussion

• What is the significance, historically and for us today, of the name "Jesus"?
• What should the title "Christ" have meant to a waiting Jewish nation? What should it mean to us?
• Why can Christ rightfully claim authority to rule your life?

7

His Only Son

When you hear a young man introduced as "my only son" you know he is the apple of his father's eye. The words reveal affection. When the Creed calls Jesus God's "only Son" (echoing "only begotten" in John 1:18; 3:16, 18) the implication is the same. Jesus, as God's only Son, enjoys his Father's dearest love. God said so himself when speaking from heaven to identify Jesus at his baptism and transfiguration: "This is my beloved Son . . . " (Matthew 3:17; 17:5).

Fully God

Moreover, this phrase of the Creed is a bulwark against such lowering and denial of Jesus' deity as one finds in Unitarianism and the cults. Jesus was not just a God-inspired good man: nor was he a super-angel, first and finest of all creatures, called "god" by courtesy because he is far above men (which is what Arians said in the fourth century, and Jehovah's Witnesses say today). Jesus was, and remains, God's only Son, as truly and fully God as his Father is. God's will, said Jesus, is that "all may honor the Son, even as they honor the Father" (John 5:23), a statement which knocks Unitarianism flat.

But is it not mere mythology to talk of a Father-Son relationship within the Godhead? No; for Jesus himself talked this way. He

<50>

called God "my Father," and himself (not "*a*" but) "*the* Son." He spoke of a unique and eternal Father-Son relation, into which he had come to bring others. "No one knows the Father except the Son and any one to whom the Son chooses to reveal him" (Matthew 11:27).

Begotten

"Begotten of his Father before all worlds . . . begotten, not made" says the Nicene Creed. This is the language of fourth-century debate. The point of it is that though the Son lives his life in dependence on the Father, because that is his nature ("I live because of the Father," John 6:57), he is in himself divine and eternal, and is not a created being. The phrase is not suggesting that the Son originated after the Father, or is in himself less than the Father.

"Begotten" in John's adjective "only begotten" cannot signify an event in God's past which is not also part of his present, since it is only for us creatures who live in time that momentary events exist. Time as we know it is part of creation, and its Maker is not subject to its limitations, any more than he is subject to the limitations of created space. For us, life is a sequence of moments, and future and past events (begettings, or any other) are both out of reach; but to God (so we must suppose, though we cannot imagine it) all events are constantly present in an eternal Now.

So the pre-mundane "begetting" of the Son (as distinct from the temporal and metaphorical "begetting" of the king in Psalm 2:7, which is applied to Christ in Acts 13:33 and Hebrews 1:5, 5:5, and which means simply bringing him to the throne) must be thought of not as a momentary event whereby God, after being singular, became plural, but as an eternal relationship whereby the first person is always Father to the Son and the second is always Son to the Father. In the third century Origen happily expressed this thought by speaking of the "eternal generation" of the Son. It is part of the unique glory of the triune God.

Mystery

Formulae for the incarnation—the Council of Chalcedon's "one person in two natures, fully God and fully man," or Karl Barth's "God for man, and man for God"—sound simple, but the thing itself is unfathomable. It is easy to shoot down the ancient heresies that the Son took a human body without a human soul, or that he was always two persons under one skin, and with them the modern heresy that the "enfleshing" of the Son was merely a special case of the indwelling of the Spirit, so that Jesus was not God, but merely a God-filled man—but to grasp what the incarnation was in positive terms is beyond us. Don't worry, though; you do not need to know how God became man in order to know Christ! Understand it or not, the fact remains that "the Word became flesh" (John 1:14); it was the supreme, mind-blowing miracle; love prompted it; and our part is not to speculate about it and scale it down, but to wonder and adore and love and exalt "Jesus Christ... the same yesterday and today and for ever" (Hebrews 13:8).

Answer thy mercy's whole design,
My God incarnated for me;
My spirit make the radiant shrine,
My light and full salvation be;
And through the shades of death unknown
Conduct me to thy dazzling throne.

Further Bible Study

God's incarnate Son:
- Colossians 1:13-23

Questions for Thought and Discussion

- Why is it not enough to call Jesus God-inspired, a superior angel, or even a god?
- What is the significance of the fact that the Son is not a created being?
- Why does facing Christianity mean facing up to Jesus Christ?

8

Born of the Virgin Mary

The Bible says that the Son of God entered and left this world by acts of supernatural power. His exit was by resurrection-plus-ascension, and his entry by virgin birth: both fulfilling Old Testament anticipations (see Isaiah 7:14 for the virgin birth, and 53:10-12 for resurrection-ascension).

The entry and exit miracles carry the same message. First, they confirm that Jesus, though not less than man, was more than man. His earthly life, though fully human, was also divine. He, the co-creator, was in this world—his own world—as a visitor; he came from God, and went to God.

The Fathers appealed to the virgin birth as proof, not that Jesus was truly divine as distinct from being merely human, but that he was truly human as distinct from merely looking human as ghosts and angels might do, and it was probably as a witness against *docetism* (as this view was called) that the virgin birth was included in the Creed. But it witnesses against *humanitarianism* (the view that Jesus was just a fine man) with equal force.

Second, these two miracles indicate Jesus' freedom from sin. Virgin-born, he did not inherit the guilty twist called original sin:

his manhood was untainted, and his acts, attitudes, motives, and desires were consequently faultless. The New Testament emphasizes his sinlessness (see John 8:29, 46; Romans 5:18ff.; 2 Corinthians 5:21; Hebrews 4:15; 7:26; 1 Peter 2:22-24; etc.). Being sinless, he could not be held by death once his sacrifice was done.

Two Stories

The New Testament gives two complementary accounts of the virgin birth, evidently independent yet strikingly harmonious—Joseph's story in Matthew 1 and Mary's in Luke 1, 2. Both show every sign of being sober history. Ancient historians, seeing themselves as artists and moralists, usually omitted reference to sources, but Luke drops a broad hint that he had Mary's narrative firsthand (cf. 2:51 with 1:1-3).

Matthew and Luke give two genealogies of Jesus (Matthew 1:2-17; Luke 3:23-38), which has puzzled some, but there are at least two straightforward ways of harmonizing them. Either Luke's genealogy gives Mary's line, but starts with Joseph as Jesus' putative father (verse 23) because it was standard practice to declare descent through males, or else Luke traces Joseph's biological descent as distinct from the royal line of succession which Matthew appears to follow throughout. (See Prof. F. F. Bruce, "Genealogy of Jesus Christ," in *The New Bible Dictionary* for the details.)

Skepticism

For the past century and a half skepticism about both Jesus' virgin birth and his physical resurrection has been quite unreasonably strong. It began as part of a rationalistic quest for a non-miraculous Christianity, and though that quest is now out of fashion (and a good thing too) the skepticism lingers on, clinging to the minds of Christian people as the smell of cigarettes clings to the room after the ashtrays have been cleared. It is no doubt possible (though it is neither easy nor natural) to believe in the incarnation of the eternal, pre-existing Son while disbelieving the entry and exit miracles; greater inconsistencies have been known; but it is much more logical, indeed the only reasonable course, to hold that since on other grounds we acknowledge Jesus and the Word made flesh, these two miracles, as elements in the larger miracle of the Son's incarnate life, raise no special difficulty.

Certainly, if we deny the virgin birth because it was a miracle, we should in logic deny Jesus' bodily resurrection too. These miracles are on a par, and it is unreasonable to accept either while rejecting the other.

Mary was a virgin till after Jesus' birth, but later ideas of her perpetual virginity are merely fanciful. The gospels show that Jesus had brothers and sisters (Mark 3:31; 6:3).

"Conceived by the Holy Spirit, born of the Virgin Mary" in the Creed witnesses to the reality of the Incarnation, not the glory of Jesus' mother: the Roman Catholic Church, however, has sponsored the unhappy development of Mariology (Mary-doctrine) among theologians and Mariolatry (Mary-worship) among the faithful. Mariology, which sees Mary as co-redeemer, rests on the nonbiblical teaching that Mary, like Jesus, was born without sin (the immaculate conception) and entered resurrection glory straight after death (the assumption).

But the real Mary, the Mary of Scripture, saw herself simply as a saved sinner. "My spirit hath rejoiced in God my Saviour" (Luke 1:47, KJV). She sets us a marvelous example, not just of the privilege (and the price!) of cooperating in God's plan to bless the world (see Luke 1:38; 2:35), but also of humble response to God's grace. Parents are slow to take things from their children, and Jesus himself commented sadly at one stage that "a prophet is not without honor except . . . in his own house" (Matthew 13:57); but Mary and her family, after initial disbelief (cf. Matthew 13:57; Mark 3:20ff., 31-35; John 7:3-5), came to living faith in her son (Acts 1:14). Have we learned from their example?

Further Bible Study

The virgin birth:
- Matthew 1:1-25
- Luke 1:26-56

49

Questions for Thought and Discussion

- What do the miracles associated with Christ's earthly entry and exit show us about him?
- Do you agree that one's attitude toward the virgin birth and the resurrection of Jesus should be the same?
- How does the biblical picture of Mary compare with that traditionally given by the Roman Catholic Church?

9

Suffered under Pontius Pilate

Fancy a school of scientists or philosophers, or the members of a political party, constantly repeating that their founder was put to death by the government, as a threat to law and order! Yet this is what Christians do, and the cross of Jesus is the centerpiece of the Creed. "Suffered under Pontius Pilate, was crucified." Look at these words in reverse order.

"Was crucified." This was the standard Roman way of executing criminals. To say "Jesus was crucified" is like saying he was hanged, or went to the electric chair.

Pilate

"Under Pontius Pilate." Hitler will be remembered as the man who gassed the Jews, and Pilate, a nonentity otherwise, goes down in history as the man who killed Jesus. Under the Roman occupation, the Jewish authorities could not execute anyone, so when they had passed sentence on Jesus for confessing his true identity as God's savior-king, the Christ (they thought the confession blasphemous), they passed him on to the governor for action.

Pilate, having symbolically washed his hands of the matter—the goofiest gesture, perhaps, of all time—gave the green light for judicial murder, directing that Jesus, though guiltless, should die all the same to keep people happy. Pilate saw this as shrewd government; how cynical can you get?

Passion

"Suffered." This word carries not only the everyday meaning of bearing pain, but also the older and wider sense of being the object affected by someone else's action. The Latin is *passus*, whence the noun "passion." Both God and men were agents of Jesus' passion: "this Jesus, delivered up according to the plan and foreknowledge of God, you crucified and killed by the hands of lawless men" (Acts 2:23, from Peter's first sermon). God's purpose at the cross was as real as was the guilt of the crucifiers.

What was God's purpose? Judgment on sin, for the sake of mercy to sinners. The miscarrying of human justice was the doing of divine justice. Jesus knew on the cross all the pain, physical and mental, that man could inflict and also the divine wrath and rejection that my sins deserve; for he was there in my place, making atonement for me. "All we like sheep have gone astray . . . and the Lord has laid on him the iniquity of us all" (Isaiah 53:6).

> *Because the sinless Saviour died*
> *My sinful soul is counted free;*
> *For God, the Just, is satisfied*
> *To look on him—and pardon me.*

Propitiation

Here we reach the real heart—the heart of the heart, we may say—of Christianity; for if the incarnation is its shrine, the Atonement is certainly its holy of holies. If the incarnation was the supreme miracle, it was yet only the first of a series of steps down from the joy and bliss of heaven to the pain and shame of Calvary (Philippians 2:5-8). The reason why the Son of God became man was to shed his blood as (in the Prayer Book's words) "a full, perfect, and sufficient sacrifice, oblation, and satisfaction, for the sins of the whole world." God "did not spare his own Son, but gave him up for us all" (Romans 8:32): that was the measure of his love (cf. 5:5-8).

It is in the same terms—terms, that is, not of tolerant avuncular benevolence, but of this particular precious gift—that John explains what he means by his great and glorious, but much-misunderstood, declaration, "*God is love*." "In this is love," he explains, "not that we loved God but that [when we didn't] he loved us and sent his Son to be the expiation [better, propitiation] for our sins" (1 John 4:8-10).

The cross of Christ has many facets of meaning. As our sacrifice for sins, it was *propitiation* (Romans 3:25; 1 John 2:2, 4:10; cf. Hebrews 2:17); that is, a means of quenching God's personal penal wrath against us by blotting out our sins from his sight. ("Expiation" in the RSV rendering of these texts signifies only "a means of blotting out sins," which is an inadequate translation.) As our propitiation, it was *reconciliation*, the making of peace for us with our offended, estranged, angry Creator (Romans 5:9-11). We are not wise to play down God's hostility against us sinners; what we should do is magnify our Savior's achievement for us in displacing wrath by peace.

Again, as our reconciliation, the cross was *redemption*, rescue from bondage and misery by the payment of a price (see Ephesians 1:7; Romans 3:24; Revelation 5:9; Mark 10:45); and as redemption, it was *victory* over all hostile powers that had kept us, and wanted still to keep us, in sin and out of God's favor (Colossians 2:13-15). All these angles must be explored if we are to grasp the whole truth.

"The Son of God . . . loved me, and gave himself for me"; so "God forbid that I should glory, save in the cross of our Lord Jesus Christ" (Galatians 2:20; 6:14, KJV). So said Paul. Thank God, I can identify. Can you?

Further Bible Study

The meaning of the cross:
- Isaiah 53
- Romans 3:19-26
- Hebrews 10:1-25

Questions for Thought and Discussion
- What is the full meaning which Christians find in the word "suffered" (Latin passus)?
- "Both God and men were agents of Jesus' passion." Explain.
- What does Christ's death have to do with your sins?

10

He Descended
into Hell

Death has been called "the new obscenity," the nasty thing which no polite person nowadays will talk about in public. But death, even when unmentionable, remains inescapable. The one sure fact of life is that one day, with or without warning, quietly or painfully, it is going to stop. How will I, then, cope with death when my turn comes?

Christian Victory

Christians hold that the Jesus of the Scriptures is alive, and that those who know him as Savior, Lord, and Friend find in this knowledge a way through all life's problems, dying included. For "Christ leads me through no darker rooms/Than he went through before." Having tasted death himself, he can support us while we taste it, and carry us through the great change to share the life beyond death into which he himself has passed. Death without Christ is "the king of terrors," but death with Christ loses the "sting," the power to hurt, which it otherwise would have.

John Preston, the Puritan, knew this. When he lay dying, they asked him if he feared death, now it was so close. "No," whispered

Preston; "I shall change my *place*, but I shall not change my *company*." As if to say: I shall leave my friends, but not my Friend, for he will never leave me.

This is victory—victory over death, and the fear it brings. And it is to point the way to this victory that the Creed, before announcing Jesus' resurrection, declares: "he descended into hell." Though this clause did not establish itself in the Creed till the fourth century, and is therefore not used by some churches, what it says is of very great importance, as we can now see.

Hades, not Gehenna

The English is misleading, for "hell" has changed its sense since the English form of the Creed was fixed. Originally, "hell" meant the place of the departed as such, corresponding to the Greek *Hades* and the Hebrew *Sheol.* That is what it means here, where the Creed echoes Peter's statement that Psalm 16:10, "thou wilt not abandon my soul to *Hades*" (so RSV: AV has "hell"), was a prophecy fulfilled when Jesus rose (see Acts 2:27-31). But since the seventeenth century "hell" has been used to signify only the state of final retribution for the godless, for which the New Testament name is *Gehenna.*

What the Creed means, however, is that Jesus entered, not *Gehenna*, but *Hades*—that is, that he really died, and that it was from a genuine death, not a simulated one, that he rose.

Perhaps it should be said (though one shrinks from laboring something so obvious) that "descended" does *not* imply that the way from Palestine to Hades is down into the ground, any more than "rose" implies that Jesus returned to surface level up the equivalent of a mine shaft! The language of descent is used because Hades, being the place of the disembodied, is *lower* in worth and dignity than is life on earth, where body and soul are together and humanity is in that sense whole.

Jesus in Hades

"Being put to death in the flesh but made alive in the spirit" (1 Peter 3:18), Jesus entered Hades, and Scripture tells us briefly what he did there.

First, by his presence he made Hades into Paradise (a place of pleasure) for the penitent thief (cf. Luke 23:43), and presumably for all others who died trusting him during his earthly ministry, just as he does now for the faithful departed (see Philippians 1:21-23; 2 Corinthians 5:6-8).

Second, he perfected the spirits of Old Testament believers (Hebrews 12:23; cf. 11:40), bringing them out of the gloom which Sheol, the "pit," had hitherto been for them (cf. Psalm 88:3-6, 10-12), into this same Paradise experience. This is the core of truth in Medieval fantasies of the "harrowing of hell."

Third, 1 Peter 3:19 tells us that he "made proclamation" (presumably, of his kingdom and appointment as the world's judge) to the imprisoned "spirits" who had rebelled in antediluvian times (presumably, the fallen angels of 2 Peter 2:4 ff., who are also the "sons of God" of Genesis 6:1-4). Some have based on this one text a hope that all humans who did not hear the gospel in this life, or who having heard it rejected it, will have it savingly preached to them in the life to come, but Peter's words do not provide the least warrant for the inference.

What makes Jesus' entry into Hades important for us is not, however, any of this, but simply the fact that now we can face death knowing that when it comes we shall not find ourselves alone. He has been there before us, and he will see us through.

Further Bible Study

The Christian's attitude toward death:
- Philippians 1:19-26
- 2 Corinthians 5:1-10
- 2 Timothy 4:6-18

Questions for Thought and Discussion

- Define and differentiate the biblical terms Hades, Sheol, Gehenna.
- How do we know that Christ's experience of death was genuine? What is the importance of this fact?
- What difference does it make whether we face death with Christ or without him?

11

The Third Day

Suppose that Jesus, having died on the cross, had stayed dead. Suppose that, like Socrates or Confucius, he was now no more than a beautiful memory. Would it matter? We should still have his example and teaching; wouldn't they be enough?

Jesus' Rising is Crucial

Enough for what? Not for Christianity. Had Jesus not risen, but stayed dead, the bottom would drop out of Christianity, for four things would then be true.

First, to quote Paul, 1 Corinthians 15:17: "if Christ has not been raised, your faith is futile and you are still in your sins."

Second, there is then no hope of our rising either; we must expect to stay dead too.

Third, if Jesus Christ is not risen, then he is not reigning and will not return and every single item in the Creed after "suffered and was buried" will have to be struck out.

Fourth, Christianity cannot be what the first Christians thought it was—fellowship with a living Lord who is identical with the Jesus of the Gospels. The Jesus of the Gospels can still be your hero, but he cannot be your Savior.

A Fact of History

To show that it views Jesus' resurrection as fact of history, the Creed actually times it—"the third day," counting inclusively (the ancients' way) from the day when Jesus was "crucified under Pontius Pilate" in about A.D. 30. On that precise day, in Jerusalem, capital of Palestine, Jesus came alive and vacated a rock tomb, and death was conquered for all time.

Can we be sure it happened? The evidence is solid. The tomb was empty, and nobody could produce the body. For more than a month after, the disciples kept meeting Jesus alive, always unexpectedly, usually in groups (from two to 500). Hallucinations don't happen this way!

The disciples, for their part, were sure that the risen Christ was no fancy, and tirelessly proclaimed his rising in face of ridicule, persecution, and even death—a most effective way of scotching the malicious rumor that they stole Jesus' body (cf. Matthew 28:11-15).

The corporate experience of the Christian church over nineteen centuries chimes in with the belief that Jesus rose, for the risen Lord truly "walks with me and talks with me along life's narrow way," and communion with him belongs to the basic Christian awareness of reality.

No sense can be made of any of this evidence save by supposing that Jesus really rose.

Well might Prof. C. F. D. Moule issue his challenge: "If the coming into existence of the Nazarenes, a phenomenon undeniably attested in the New Testament, rips a great hole in history, a hole of the size and shape of the resurrection, what does the secular historian propose to stop it up with?" The actual historical effect is inconceivable without the resurrection of Jesus as its objective historical cause.

Facing the Evidence

A Christian in public debate accused his skeptical opponent of having more faith than he—"for," he said, "in face of the evidence, I can't believe that Jesus did not rise, and you can!" It really is harder to disbelieve the resurrection than to accept it, much harder. Have you yet seen it that way? To believe in Jesus Christ as Son of God and living Savior, and to echo the words of ex-doubter Thomas, "My Lord and my God," is certainly more than an exercise of reason, but in the face of the evidence it is the only *reasonable* thing a person can do.

What Jesus' Rising Means

What is the significance of Jesus' rising? In a word, it marked Jesus out as Son of God (Romans 1:4); it vindicated his righteousness (John 16:10); it demonstrated victory over death (Acts 2:24); it guaranteed the believer's forgiveness and justification (1 Corinthians 15:17; Romans 4:25), and his own future resurrection too (1 Corinthians 15:18); and it brings him into the reality of resurrection life now (Romans 6:4). Marvelous! You could speak of Jesus' rising as the most hopeful—hope-full—thing that has ever happened—and you would be right!

Further Bible Study

The resurrection of Jesus:
- John 20:1-18
- 1 Corinthians 15:1-28

Questions for Thought and Discussion

- How would Christianity be different if Christ had not risen?
- What evidence is there for Jesus' resurrection?
- Why does Packer speak of believing that Christ rose as "the only reasonable thing a person can do"? Do you agree?

12

He Ascended
into Heaven

He ascended" echoes Jesus' "I ascend" (John 20:17; compare 6:62). "Into heaven" echoes "taken up from you into heaven," the angels' words in the Ascension story (Acts 1:10). But what is "heaven"? Is it the sky, or outer space? Does the Creed mean that Jesus was the first astronaut? No, both it and the Bible are making a different point.

What Heaven Means

"Heaven" in the Bible means three things: 1. The endless, self-sustaining life of God. In this sense, God always dwelt "in heaven," even when there was no earth. 2. The state of angels or men as they share the life of God, whether in foretaste now or in fullness hereafter. In this sense, the Christian's reward, treasure, and inheritance are all "in heaven" and heaven is shorthand for the Christian's final hope. 3. The sky, which, being above us and more like infinity than anything else we know, is an emblem in space and time of God's eternal life, just as the rainbow is an emblem of his everlasting covenant (see Genesis 9:8-17).

Bible and Creed proclaim that in the Ascension, forty days after his rising, Jesus entered heaven in sense 2 in a new and momentous way: thenceforth he "sitteth on the right hand of God the Father almighty," ruling all things in his Father's name and with his Father's almightiness for the long-term good of his people. "On the right hand of God" signifies not a palatial location but a regal function: see Acts 2:33ff.; Romans 8:34; Ephesians 1:20ff.; Hebrews 1:3, 13; 10:12ff.; 12:2. He "ascended far above the heavens" (that is, reentered his pre-incarnate life, a life unrestricted by anything created) "that he might fill all things" (that is, make his kingly power effective everywhere; see Ephesians 4:10). "Ascended" is, of course, a picture-word implying exaltation ("going up!") to a condition of supreme dignity and power.

The Ascension

What happened at the Ascension, then, was not that Jesus became a spaceman, but that his disciples were shown a sign, just as at the Transfiguration. As C. S. Lewis put it, "they saw first a short vertical movement and then a vague luminosity (that is what 'cloud' presumably means . . .) and then nothing." In other words, Jesus' final withdrawal from human sight, to rule till he returns to judgment, was presented to the disciples' outward eyes as a going up into heaven in sense 3. This should not puzzle us. Withdrawal had to take place somehow, and going up, down, or sideways, failing to appear or suddenly vanishing were the only possible ways. Which would signify most clearly that Jesus would henceforth be reigning in glory? That answers itself.

So the message of the Ascension story is: "Jesus the Savior reigns!"

Our Hearts in Heaven

In a weary world in which grave philosophers were counseling suicide as man's best option, the unshakable, rollicking optimism of the first Christians, who went on feeling on top of the world however much the world seemed to be on top of them, made a vast impression. (It still does, when Christians are Christian enough to show it!) Three certainties were, and are, its secret.

The first concerns God's *world*. It is that Christ really rules it, that he has won a decisive victory over the dark powers that had mastered it, and that the manifesting of this fact is only a matter of time. God's war with Satan is now like a chess game in which the result is sure but the losing player has not yet given up, or like the last phase of human hostilities in which the defeated enemy's counter-attacks, though fierce and frequent, cannot succeed, and are embraced in the victor's strategy as mere mopping-up operations. One wishes that our reckoning of dates "A.D." (*anno Domini*, in the year of our Lord), which starts in intention (though probably a few years too late) with Jesus' birth, had been calculated from the year of the cross, resurrection, and ascension; for that was when Jesus' Lordship became the cosmic fact that it is today.

The second certainty concerns God's *Christ*. It is that our reigning Lord "intercedes" for us (Romans 8:34; Hebrews 7:25), in the sense that he appears "in the presence of God" as our "advocate" (Hebrews 9:24; 1 John 2:1) to ensure that we receive "grace to help" in our need (Hebrews 4:16) and so are kept to the end in the love of God (cf. the Good Shepherd's pledge, John 10:27-29). "Intercede" denotes, not a suppliant making an appeal to charity, but the intervening of one who has sovereign right and power to make requests and take action in another's interest. It is truly said that our Lord's presence and life in heaven as the enthroned priest-king, our propitiation, so to speak, in person, is itself his interces-sion: just for him to be there guarantees all grace to us, and glory too.

An eighteenth-century jingle puts this certainty into words which make the heart leap:

Love moved thee to die;
And on this I rely,
My Saviour hath loved me, I cannot tell why:
But this I can find,
We two are so joined
He'll not be in glory and leave me behind.

The third certainty concerns God's *people*. It is a matter of God-given experience, as well as of God-taught understanding. It is that Christians enjoy here and now a hidden life of fellowship with the Father and the Son which nothing, not even death itself, can touch—for it is the life of the world to come begun already, the life of heaven tasted here on earth. The explanation of this experience, which all God's people know in some measure, is that believers have actually passed through death (not as a physical, but as a personal and psychic, event) into the eternal life which lies beyond. "You have died, and your life is hid with Christ in God" (Colossians 3:3; cf. 2:12; Romans 6:3, 4). "God . . . when we were dead . . . made us alive together with Christ . . . and raised us up with him, and made us sit with him in the heavenly places in Christ Jesus" (Ephesians 2:4ff.).

The prayer used on Ascension Day in the Anglican Prayer Book prays God to "grant . . . that like as we do believe thy only-begotten Son our Lord Jesus Christ to have ascended into heavens; so we may also in heart and mind thither ascend, and with him continually dwell." May we be enabled, in the power of these three certainties, to do just that.

Further Bible Study

The significance of the Ascension:
- Acts 1:1-11
- Ephesians 1:15-2:10

Questions for Thought and Discussion

- In what sense did Jesus ascend to heaven?
- To what did he return?
- What is Christ doing now? What importance has this heavenly ministry for us?

13

He Shall Come

The core of the Creed is its witness to the past, present, and future of Jesus Christ: his birth, death, rising, and ascension in the past; his reign now; and his coming at a future date to judge. ("Quick" in "the quick and the dead," by the way, means living, not fast-moving.) With his coming, Scripture tells us, will come our bodily resurrection and the full everlasting life of which the Creed speaks. A new cosmic order will start then too. There's a great day coming. (See Matthew 25:14-46; John 5:25-29; Romans 8:18-24; 2 Peter 3:10-13; Revelation 20:11-21:4.)

The Christian's Hope

Nowhere does the strength of the Creed as a charter for life come out more clearly. In today's world, pessimism prevails because people lack hope. They foresee only the bomb, or bankruptcy, or a weary old age—nothing worthwhile. Communists and Jehovah's Witnesses attract by offering bright hopes of heaven on earth—following the Revolution in one case, Armageddon in the other; but Christians have a hope that outshines both—the hope of which Bunyan's Mr. Stand-fast said, "the thoughts of what I am going to . . . lie as a glowing Coal at my Heart." The Creed highlights this hope when it declares: "he shall come."

In one sense, Christ comes for every Christian at death, but the

Creed looks to the day when he will come publicly to wind up history and judge all men—Christians as Christians, accepted already, whom a "blood-bought free reward" awaits according to the faithfulness of their service; rebels as rebels, to be rejected by the Master whom they rejected first. The judgments of Jesus, "the righteous judge" (2 Timothy 4:8; compare Romans 2:5-11), will raise no moral problems.

Certain and Glorious

Some think it will never happen—but we have God's word for it, and sober scientists now tell us that an end to our world through nuclear or ecological catastrophe is a real possibility. Christ's coming is unimaginable—but man's imagination is no measure of God's power, and the Jesus who is spiritually present to millions simultaneously now can surely make himself visibly present to the risen race then. We do not know when he will come (so we must always be ready), nor how he will come (why not in the going off of a bomb?)—but "we know that when he appears we shall be like him, for we shall see him as he is" (1 John 3:2)—and that is knowledge enough! "Come, Lord Jesus" (Revelation 22:20).

Eclipsed

The hope of Christ's return thrilled the New Testament Christians, as witness over 300 references to it in the documents—on average, one every thirteen verses. But to us it is not so much exciting as embarrassing! The phrase "Cinderella of the Creed," which was once applied to the Holy Spirit, nowadays fits Christ's return much more truly. Why is it thus in eclipse? For four main reasons, it seems.

First, this is a time of *reaction* from a century and a half of intense prophetic study expressing a spirit of prayerless pessimism about the church and doom-watching detachment from the world. This spirit, and the dogmatism that went with it about both the signs and the date of Christ's coming (despite Mark 13:32 and Acts 1:7!), were quite unjustifiable, and have given the topic a bad name.

Second, this is a time of *skepticism* as to whether Christ personally and physically rose and ascended, and this naturally spawns dithering doubts as to whether we can hope ever to see him again.

Third, this is a time of *timidity*, in which Christians, while query-ing the materialistic self-sufficiency of Western secularism and Marxist ideologies, hesitate to challenge their "this-worldly" pre-occupation, lest the counter-accusation be provoked that Christians do not care about social and economic justice. So the fact that Christ will end this world, and that the best part of the Christian hope lies beyond it, gets played down.

Fourth, this is a time of *worldly-mindedness*, at least among the prosperous Christians of the West. We think less and less about the better things that Christ will bring us at his reappearance, because our thoughts are increasingly absorbed by the good things we enjoy here. No one would wish persecution or destitution on another, but who can deny that at this point they might do us good?

All four attitudes are unhealthy and unworthy. God help us to transcend them.

Be Prepared

"Be ready," said the Savior to his disciples, "for the Son of man is coming at an hour you do not expect" (Matthew 24:44). How does one get and stay ready? By keeping short accounts with God and men; by taking life a day at a time, as Jesus told us to do (Matthew 6:34); and by heeding the advice of Bishop Ken's hymn, "Live each day as if thy last." Budget and plan for an ordinary span of years, but in spirit be packed up and ready to leave at any time. This should be part of our daily devotional discipline. When the Lord comes, he should find his people praying for revival and planning world evan-gelism—but packed up and ready to leave nonetheless. If Boy Scouts can learn to live realistically in terms of the motto "Be pre-pared" for any ordinary thing that might happen, why are Christians so slow to learn the same lesson in relation to the momentous event of Christ's return?

Further Bible Study

The Christian's attitude toward Christ's return:
• Luke 12:35-48
• 1 Thessalonians 4:13-5:11
• 2 Peter 3

Questions for Thought and Discussion

• In what way is Christ's future coming reason for hope?
• When Christ returns, what will he do? What are your reactions to knowing this?
• What does the Bible not tell us about Christ's return? Why do you think God withholds this information?

14

I Believe in the Holy Spirit

I believe in the Holy Spirit": so starts the Creed's third paragraph. From the creating work of the Father and the rescue work of the Son, it turns to the re-creating work of the Spirit, whereby we are actually made new in and through Christ. So we hear of *church* (new community), *forgiveness* (new relationship), *resurrection* (new existence), and *everlasting life* (new fulfillment). But first comes a profession of faith in the Spirit himself.

The Spirit of Christ

He is divine ("holy" says this). He is an active Person, the Executive of the Godhead. Yes, but doing and aiming at what? Misbelief abounds here. Some associate the Spirit with mystical states and artistic inspirations, both Christian and pagan. Others link the Spirit only with unusual Christian experiences—feeling "high" (to use the world's word), seeking visions, receiving revelations, speaking in tongues, healing. But these are secondary elements of the Spirit's work, where they derive from the Spirit at all.

The Old Testament mentions the Spirit in connection with creation, both divine (Genesis 1:2) and human (Exodus 31:1-6); the inspiring of God's spokesmen (Isaiah 61:1; the Nicene Creed states that the Spirit "spoke by the prophets"); the equipping and enabling of God's servants (judges, kings, etc.; e.g., Judges 13:25; 14:19; Isaiah 11:2; Zechariah 4:6); and the evoking of godliness in individuals and in the community (Psalm 51:11; Ezekiel 36:26ff.; 37:1-14; Zechariah 12:10). All this gains deeper meaning in the New Testament, where the Spirit is shown to be a personal agent distinct from the Father and the Son, and is spoken of as the Spirit of Christ (Romans 8:9, 1 Peter 1:11).

The key to understanding the New Testament view of the Spirit's work is to see that his purpose is identical with the Father's—namely, to see glory and praise come to the Son. Accordingly—

First, the Spirit serviced the Son throughout his earthly life from the moment when, as the Creed says, he was "conceived by the Holy Spirit" (Matthew 1:20). The Spirit's dove-like descent on him at his baptism showed not only that he was the Spirit-giver, but also that he was himself Spirit-filled (Luke 4:1; cf. verses 14, 18). It was "through the eternal Spirit" that he offered himself in sacrifice for us (Hebrews 9:14).

Second, the Spirit now acts as Jesus' agent—"another Comforter" (helper, supporter, advocate, encourager). He shows Jesus to us through the gospel, unites us to him by faith, and indwells us to change us "into his likeness" by causing "the fruit of the Spirit" to grow in us (2 Corinthians 3:18; Galatians 5:22ff.).

"He will glorify [not himself but] me, for he will take what is mine and declare it to you" (John 16:14). Jesus' words indicate the self-effacing character of the Spirit; he functions as a floodlight trained on Christ, so that it is Christ, not the Spirit, whom we see. In the gospel message, Jesus is set before us throughout, saying: Come to me; follow me. In our conscience as we hear the gospel with the inner ear of faith, the Spirit, standing behind us as it were to throw light over our shoulder on to Jesus, constantly urges: Go to him; deal with him. So we do—and it is this that makes our life Christian.

Witness and Ministry

The Spirit is *witness* and *teacher* (1 John 5:7; 2:27; cf. 4:2ff.) inasmuch as, first, he convinces us that the Jesus of the gospel, the New

Testament Christ, really exists, and is what he is "for us men, and for our salvation"; second, he assures us that as believers we are God's children and heirs with Christ (Romans 8:16ff.); third, he moves us to bear witness to the Christ whom his witness led us to know (cf. John 15:26). What the Spirit's witnessing effects is not private revelation of something hitherto undisclosed, but personal reception of God's public testimony which was "there" all along in the Scriptures, but went unheeded. Paul is describing the Spirit's work of witness when he speaks of "having the eyes of your hearts enlightened" (Ephesians 1:18).

Third, the Spirit gives to every Christian one or more gifts (i.e., capacities to express Christ in serving God and man), so that "every-member ministry" in the church, which is Christ's body, may become a reality (1 Corinthians 12:4-7; Ephesians 4:11-16). This manifold ministry is itself Christ's own ministry continuing from heaven, through us as his hands, feet, and mouth; and the Spirit's bestowing of gifts should be seen as further servicing and glorifying of Christ on his part, inasmuch as it is the means whereby Christ's personal ministry to men is able to go on.

Signs of the Spirit

What then are the signs that Christ's self-effacing Spirit is at work? Not mystical raptures, nor visions and supposed revelations, nor even healings, tongues, and apparent miracles; for Satan, playing on our psychosomatic complexity and our fallenness, can produce all these things (cf. 2 Thessalonians 2:9ff.; Colossians 2:18). The only sure signs are that the Christ of the Bible is acknowledged, trusted, loved for his grace and served for his glory, and that believers actually turn from sin to the life of holiness which is Christ's image in his people (cf. 1 Corinthians 12:3; 2 Corinthians 3:17). These are the criteria by which we must judge, for instance, the modern "charismatic renewal," and Christian Science (reaching, perhaps, different verdicts in the two cases).

So when I say, as a Christian, "I believe in the Holy Spirit," my meaning should be, first, that I believe personal fellowship, across space and time, with the living Christ of the New Testament to be a reality, which through the Spirit I have found; second, that I am open to be led by the Spirit, who now indwells me, into Christian knowledge, obedience, and service, and I expect to be so led each day; and, third, that I bless him as the author of my assurance that I am a son and heir of God. Truly, it is a glorious thing to believe in the Holy Spirit!

Further Bible Study

The Spirit's ministry:
- John 7:37-39; 14:15-26; 16:7-15
- Romans 8:1-17

Questions for Thought and Discussion

- How does the work of the Spirit differ from that of the Father and the Son?
- What does the Holy Spirit do as "Jesus' agent"?
- What would you say to a professed Christian who doubted if he had ever experienced the ministry of the Holy Spirit?

15

The Holy
Catholic Church

It is by strict theological logic that the Creed confesses faith in the Holy Spirit before proceeding to the church, and that it speaks of the church before mentioning personal salvation (forgiveness, resurrection, everlasting life). For though Father and Son have loved the church and the Son has redeemed it, it is the Holy Spirit who actually creates it, by inducing faith; and it is in the church, through its ministry and fellowship, that personal salvation ordinarily comes to be enjoyed.

Unhappily, there is at this point a parting of the ways. Roman Catholics and Protestants both say the Creed, yet they are divided. Why? Basically, because of divergent understandings of "I believe in the holy catholic church"—"one holy catholic and apostolic church," as the true text of the Nicene Creed has it.

Roman Versus Protestant

Official Roman Catholic teaching presents the church of Christ as the *one* organized body of baptized persons who are in communion with the Pope and acknowledge the teaching and ruling authority of the episcopal hierarchy. It is *holy* because it produces saintly folk and is kept from radical sin; *catholic* because in its worldwide spread it holds the full faith in trust for everyone; and *apostolic* because its ministerial orders stem from the apostles, and its faith (including such nonbiblical items as the assumption of Mary and her immaculate conception, the Mass-sacrifice, and papal infallibility) is a sound growth from apostolic roots. Non-Roman bodies, however church-like, are not strictly part of the church at all.

Protestants challenge this from the Bible. In Scripture (they say) the church is the *one* worldwide fellowship of believing people whose Head is Christ. It is *holy* because it is consecrated to God (though it is capable nonetheless of grievous sin); it is *catholic* because it embraces all Christians everywhere; and it is *apostolic* because it seeks to maintain the apostles' doctrine unmixed. Pope, hierarchy, and extra-biblical doctrines are not merely nonessential but actually deforming; if Rome is a church (which some Reformers doubted) she is so despite the extras, not because of them. In particular, infallibility belongs to God speaking in the Bible, not to the church nor to any of its officers, and any teaching given in or by the church must be open to correction by "God's word written."[1]

Some Protestants have taken the clause "the communion of saints" which follows "the holy catholic church" as the Creed's own elucidation of what the church is; namely, Christians in fellowship with each other—just that, without regard for any particular hierarchical structure. But it is usual to treat this phrase as affirming the real union in Christ of the church "militant here in earth" with the church triumphant, as is indicated in Hebrews 12:22-24; and it may be that the clause was originally meant to signify *communion in holy things* (word, sacrament, worship, prayers), and to make the true but distinct point that in the church there is a real sharing in the life of God. The "spiritual" view of the church as being a fellowship before it is an institution can, however, be confirmed from Scripture without appeal to this phrase, whatever its sense, being needed.

The New Testament

That the New Testament presents the Protestant view is hardly open to dispute (the dispute is over whether the New Testament is final!). The church appears in trinitarian relationships, as the family of God the Father, the body of Christ the Son, and the temple (dwelling-place) of the Holy Spirit, and so long as the dominical sacraments are administered and ministerial oversight is exercised, no organizational norms are insisted on at all. The church is the supernatural society of God's redeemed and baptized people, looking back to Christ's first coming with gratitude and on to his second coming with hope. "Your life is hid with Christ in God. When Christ who is our life appears, then you also will appear with him in glory" (Colossians 3:3ff.)—such is the church's present state and future prospect. To this hope both sacraments point, baptism prefiguring final resurrection, the Lord's Supper anticipating "the marriage supper of the Lamb" (Revelation 19:9).

For the present, however, all churches (like those in Corinth, Colossae, Galatia, and Thessalonica, to look no further) are prone to err in both faith and morals, and need constant correction and re-formation at all levels (intellectual, devotional, structural, liturgical) by the Spirit through God's Word.

The evangelical theology of revival, first spelled out in the seventeenth and eighteenth centuries, and the present-day emergence of "charismatic renewal" on a worldwide scale, reminds us of something which Roman Catholic and Protestant disputers, in their concentration on doctrinal truth, tended to miss—namely, that church must always be open to the immediacy of the Spirit's Lordship, and that disorderly vigor in a congregation is infinitely preferable to a correct and tidy deadness.

The Local Church

The acid test of the church's state is what happens in the local congregation. Each congregation is a visible outcrop of the one church universal, called to serve God and men in humility and, perhaps, humiliation while living in prospect of glory. Spirit-filled for worship and witness, active in love and care for insiders and outsiders alike, self-supporting and self-propagating, each congregation is to be a spearhead of divine counterattack for the recapture of a rebel world.

Tailpiece: how is your congregation getting on?

Note:

¹*Anglican Article XX.*

Further Bible Study

The church's nature and destiny:
- 1 Peter 2
- Ephesians 2:11–4:16

Questions for Thought and Discussion

- How does the Roman Catholic use of the New Testament differ from the Protestant one? How does this affect the concept each holds of the church?
- How does Packer define "the communion of saints"? Do you agree with what he says? Why or Why not?
- What is the function of a local Christian church in relation to the universal church?

16

Forgiveness of Sins

What are *sins*? Sin, says the Westminster Shorter Catechism, is "any want of conformity unto, or transgression of, the law of God." This echoes 1 John 3:4, "sin is lawlessness." It has other aspects too. It is lawlessness in relation to God as lawgiver, rebellion in relation to God as rightful ruler, missing the mark in relation to God as our designer, guilt in relation to God as judge, and uncleanness in relation to God as the Holy One.

Sin is a perversity touching each one of us at every point in our lives. Apart from Jesus Christ, no human being has ever been free of its infection. It appears in desires as well as deeds, and motives as well as actions. The Anglican Prayer Book rightly teaches that: "We have followed too much the devices and desires of our own hearts . . . We have left undone those things which we ought to have done, and we have done those things which we ought not to have done, and (spiritually) there is no health in us."

Sin is everybody's problem in the sight of God, for he is "of purer eyes than to behold evil," and cannot *"look on wrong"* (Habakkuk 1:13). But we find life to be a moral minefield for us; and the harder we try to avoid sin the more often we find—too late—that we have stepped where we shouldn't, and been blown to pieces so far as the required love of God and our neighbor is concerned. And where does that leave us?—"for the wrath of God is revealed from heaven against all ungodliness and wickedness of men" (Romans 1:18).

The good news, however, is this—sins can be forgiven. Central to the gospel is the glorious "but" of Psalm 130:4—"If thou, O Lord, shouldst mark iniquities, Lord, who could stand? *But* there is forgiveness with thee, that thou mayest be feared"—that is, worshipped with loyalty (for that is what *fear* of God means).

Vital and Real

Forgiveness is pardon in a personal setting. It is taking back into friendship those who went against you, hurt you, and put themselves in the wrong with you. It is *compassionate* (showing unmerited kindness to the wrongdoer), *creative* (renewing the spoiled relationship)—and, inevitably, *costly*. God's forgiveness is the supreme instance of this, for it is God in love restoring fellowship at the cost of the cross.

If our sins were unforgivable, where should we be? A bad conscience is the most universal experience—and the most wretched. No outward change relieves it; you carry it with you all your waking hours. The more conscientious you are, the more your knowledge of having failed others, and God too, will haunt you. Without forgiveness you will have no peace. A bad conscience delivering at full strength, tearing you to pieces in the name of God, is hell indeed, both here and hereafter.

Luther Knew It

A man distressed about sin wrote to Luther. The Reformer, who himself had suffered long agonies over this problem, replied: "Learn to know Christ and him crucified. Learn to sing to him and say—Lord Jesus, you are my righteousness, I am your sin. You took on you what was mine; you set on me what was yours. You became what you were not that I might become what I was not." Compare Paul: "For our sake [God] made [Christ] to be sin who knew no sin, so that in him we might become the righteousness of God" (2 Corinthians 5:21). Link up with Jesus, the living Lord, by faith, and the great exchange is fulfilled. Through Jesus' atoning death God accepts you as righteous, and cancels your sins. This is justification, forgiveness, and peace.

Paul in Romans and Galatians, and the Reformers after him, spoke of justification rather than of forgiveness. This is because justification is forgiveness *plus*; it signifies not only a washing out of the past, but also acceptance and the gift of a righteous man's status for the future. Also, justification is final, being a decision on which God will never go back, and so it is the basis of assurance, whereas present forgiveness does not necessarily argue more than temporary forbearance. So justification—public acquittal and reinstatement before God's judgment-seat—is actually the richer concept.

By Faith Only

In the past (things are less clear-cut today) Roman Catholics did not grasp the decisiveness of present justification, nor see that Christ's righteousness ("my Savior's obedience and blood," as Toplady put it) is its whole ground, nor realize that our part is to stop trying to earn it, and simply take it as God's free gift of grace. So they insisted that sacraments, "good works," and purgatorial pains hereafter were all necessary means of final acceptance, because they were among the grounds on which that acceptance was based. But the Reformers preached, as Paul did, full and final acceptance through a decisive act of forgiveness here and now; and this, they said, is by faith only.

Why faith *only*? Because Christ's righteousness *only* is the basis of pardon and peace, and Christ and his gifts are received *only* by faith's embrace. Faith means not only believing God's truth, but trusting Christ, taking what he offers, and then triumphing in the knowledge of what is now yours.

Is God's gift of forgiveness by faith yours yet? It is easily missed. The Jews missed it, said Paul; their tragedy was that their zeal for God led them to try to establish their own righteousness (i.e., earn his acceptance), and "they did not submit to God's righteousness" (i.e., to his way of forgiving and justifying, by faith in Christ only): see Romans 10:2ff. The pathetic truth is that we sinners are self-righteous to the core, and we are constantly justifying ourselves, and we hate admitting that there is anything seriously wrong with us, anything that God or man might seriously hold against us; and we have to do violence to our own perverted instincts at this point before faith is possible for us. God save us all from repeating the tragedy of the Jews in our own lives.

Further Bible Study

Justification through Christ by faith apart from works:
- Romans 5; 10:1-13
- Galatians 2:15—3:29
- Philippians 3:4-16

Questions for Thought and Discussion

- What is forgiveness, and what does it do for the forgiven on a personal level?
- What did Luther mean by saying, "You became what you were not that I might become what I was not"?
- Why is it that forgiveness comes through faith only?

17

Resurrection of
the Body

Scripture sees death—life's one certainty—not as a friend but as a destroyer. When my body and soul separate, I shall only be a shadow of what I was. My body is part of me, the apparatus of my self-expression; without it, all my power to make things, do things, and relate to my fellows is gone. Think of someone with full use of his faculties, and compare him with a paralytic; now compare the paralytic with someone totally disembodied, and you will see what I mean. Paralytics can do little enough; disembodied persons, less still. Thus death, while not ending our existence, nullifies and in a real sense destroys it.

Coping with Death

Death is the fundamental human problem, for if death is really final then nothing is worthwhile save self-indulgence. "If the dead are not raised, let us eat and drink, for tomorrow we die" (1 Corinthians 15:32). And no philosophy or religion which cannot come to terms with death is any real use to us.

Here, however, Christianity stands out. Alone among the world's faiths and "isms" it views death as conquered. For Christian faith is hope resting on fact—namely, the fact that Jesus rose bodily from the grave and now lives eternally in heaven. The hope is that when Jesus comes back—the day when history stops and this world ends—he will "change our lowly body to be like his glorious body" (Philippians 3:21; cf. 1 John 3:2). This hope embraces all who have died in Christ as well as Christians alive at his appearing: "for the hour is coming when all who are in the tombs will hear [Jesus'] voice and come forth, those who have done good, to the resurrection of life" (John 5:28ff.). And the raising of the *body* means the restoring of the *person*—not just part of me, but all of me—to active, creative, undying life, for God and with God.

New Body

In raising believers, God completes their redemption by the gift, not of their old bodies somehow patched up, but of new bodies fit for new men. Through regeneration and sanctification God has already renewed us inwardly; now we receive bodies to match. The new body is linked with the old, yet different from it, just as plants are linked with, yet different from, the seeds from which they grew (see 1 Corinthians 15:35-44). My present body—"brother ass," as Francis of Assisi would have me call it—is like a student's old jalopy; care for it as I will, it goes precariously and never very well, and often lets me and my Master down (very frustrating!). But my new body will feel and behave like a Rolls-Royce, and then my service will no longer be spoiled.

No doubt, like me, you both love your body because it is part of you and get mad at the way it limits you. So we should. And it is good to know that God's aim in giving us second-rate physical frames here is to prepare us for managing better bodies hereafter. As C. S. Lewis says somewhere, they give you unimpressive horses to learn to ride on, and only when you are ready for it are you allowed an animal that will gallop and jump.

A dwarf I knew would weep for joy at the thought of the body God had in store for him on resurrection day, and when I think of other Christians known to me who in one way or another are physical wrecks—deformed, decaying, crippled, hormonally unbalanced, or otherwise handicapped—I can weep too for this particular element of joy which will be theirs—and yours—and mine when that day dawns.

Soul and Body

This bit of the Creed was probably put in to ward off the idea (very common for three centuries after Christ, and not unknown today) that man's hope is immortality for his soul, which (so it was thought) would be much better off disembodied. There was a tag, "the body is a tomb," which summed up this view. But it shows a wrong view both of matter (which God made, and likes, and declares good) and of man (who is not a noble soul able to excuse the shameful things he does by blaming them on to his uncouth material shell, but a psycho-physical unit whose moral state is directly expressed by his physical behavior). The disordering effect of sin is very clear in the way my physical appetites function (not to look further); but for all that these appetites are part of me and I must acknowledge moral responsibility for whatever active expression they find. The Bible doctrine of judgment is that each of us receives "good or evil, according to what he has done in the body" (2 Corinthians 5:10).

Like Christ

The promise that one day we shall have bodies "like his glorious body" (Philippians 3:20ff.) challenges us—do we really, from our hearts, welcome and embrace our promised destiny of being like Christ? (Cf. 1 John 3:2ff.) Facing this question could be a moment of truth for us. For some find their whole identity in gratifying physical itches (for sexual excitement, sleep, food, exercise, violence, alcoholic or drug-induced "highs," or whatever) and feel— alas, with too much truth—that were they deprived of these nothing would be left of them but an ache; and they see Jesus, who was not led by physical itches, as the "pale Galilean" through whose breath, according to Swinburne, the world grew cold, and whom D. H. Lawrence wanted to humanize (I have to use that verb in fairness to Lawrence, though it is the wackiest nonsense I have ever written) by imagining for him a sex life with a pagan priestess. Such a vision makes the idea of being like Jesus—that, and no more—

sound like being sentenced to a living death. Now is that how, deep down, it sounds to you?

If so, only one thing can be said. Ask God to show you how Jesus' life, body and soul, was the only fully human life that has ever been lived, and keep looking at Jesus, as you meet him in the Gospels, till you can see it. Then the prospect of being like him—that, and no less—will seem to you the noblest and most magnificent destiny possible, and by embracing it you will become a true disciple. But until you see it—please believe me: I kid you not—there is no hope for you at all.

Further Bible Study

The resurrection hope:
- Mark 12:18-27
- 1 Corinthians 15:35-58
- Philippians 3:4-16

Questions for Thought and Discussion

- Why is a religion that does not deal with death valueless to us?
- What evidence does the Bible give to show that death has been conquered?
- How much can we say that we know about the state of the resurrected?

18

The Life Everlasting

Skeptics like Fred Hoyle and Bertrand Russell have told us that the thought of an endless future life horrifies them; for (they said) it would be so boring! Evidently they have found this life boring, and cannot imagine how human existence could be made permanently interesting and worthwhile. Poor fellows! Here we see the blighting effects of godlessness, and the black pessimism to which it leads.

But not all moderns are like Hoyle and Russell. Some are anxious to survive death. Hence their interest in spiritist phenomena, supposed to give proof of survival. But three facts should be noted. First, "messages" from the departed are distressingly trivial and self-absorbed. Second, "messages" do not come from those who in this life walked close to God. Third, mediums and their "controls" are embarrassed by the name of Jesus. These facts give warning that the spiritist phenomena, whatever their true explanation, are a blind alley for investigating "the blessed hope of everlasting life."

Jesus' Presence Makes Heaven

When the Creed speaks of "*the* life everlasting" it means, not just endless existence (demons and lost souls have that), but the final joy into which Jesus entered (Hebrews 12:2), and which he promised and prayed that his followers would one day share. "Where I am, there shall my servant be also; if any one serves me, the Father will honor him." "Father, I desire that they also, whom thou hast given me, may be with me where I am, to behold my glory" (John 12:26; 17:24).

Being with Jesus is the essence of heaven; it is what the life everlasting is all about. "I have formerly lived by hearsay and faith," said Bunyan's Mr. Stand-fast, "but now I go where I shall live by sight, and shall be with him, in whose company I delight myself." What shall we do in heaven? Not lounge around!—but worship, work, think, and communicate, enjoying activity, beauty, people, and God. First and foremost, however, we shall see and love Jesus, our Savior, Master, and Friend.

Endless Joy

The everlastingness of this life was spelled out in the vividest possible way by the anonymous benefactor who appended to John Newton's "Amazing Grace" this extra verse:

When we've been there ten thousand years,
Bright shining as the sun,
We've no less days to sing God's praise
Than when we first begun.

I have been writing with enthusiasm, for this everlasting life is something to which I look forward. Why? Not because I am out of love with life here—just the reverse! My life is full of joy, from four sources—knowing God, and people, and the good and pleasant things that God and men under God have created, and doing things which are worthwhile for God or others, or for myself as God's man. But my reach exceeds my grasp. My relationships with God and others are never as rich and full as I want them to be, and I am always finding more than I thought was there in great music, great verse, great books, great lives, and the great kaleidoscope of the natural order.

As I get older, I find that I appreciate God, and people, and good and lovely and noble things, more and more intensely; so it is pure delight to think that this enjoyment will continue and increase in some form (what form, God knows, and I am content to wait and see), literally forever. Christians inherit in fact the destiny which fairy tales envisage in fancy: *we* (yes, you and I, the silly saved sinners) *live*, and live *happily*, and by God's endless mercy will live happily *ever after*.

We cannot visualize heaven's life, and the wise man will not try. Instead, he will dwell on the doctrine of heaven, which is that there the redeemed find all their heart's desire: joy with their Lord, joy with his people, and joy in the ending of all frustration and distress and the supply of all wants. What was said to the child—"If you want sweets and hamsters in heaven, they'll be there"—was not an evasion, but a witness to the truth that in heaven no felt needs or longings go unsatisfied. What our wants will actually be, however, we hardly know, save that first and foremost we shall want to be "always . . . with the Lord" (1 Thessalonians 4:17).

Often now we say in moments of great enjoyment, "I don't want this ever to stop"—but it does. Heaven, however, is different. May heaven's joys be yours, and mine.

Further Bible Study

Our destination:
● Revelation 21:1–22:5

Questions for Thought and Discussion

● Why is Packer suspicious of spiritist phenomena?
● Why will heaven be delightful? Do you personally expect and look forward to heaven? Why or why not?
● What will the residents of heaven do?

Part Two

Entering In:
Baptism and Conversion

Baptism and Conversion

"Go therefore and make disciples of all nations, baptizing them in the name of the Father and of the Son and of the Holy Spirit" (Matthew 28:19).

"And Peter said to them, 'Repent, and be baptized every one of you in the name of Jesus Christ for the forgiveness of your sins; and you shall receive the gift of the Holy Spirit'" (Acts 2:38).

"'... to open their eyes that they may turn from darkness to light and from the power of Satan to God, that they may receive forgiveness of sins and a place among those who are sanctified by faith in me'" (Acts 26:18).

"'If I do not wash you,' Jesus replied, 'you are not in fellowship with me'" (John 13:8, NEB).

"Do you not know that all of us who have been baptized into Christ Jesus were baptized into his death? We were buried therefore with him by baptism into death, so that as Christ was raised from the dead by the glory of the Father, we too might walk in newness of life. For if we have been united with him in a death like his, we shall certainly be united with him in a resurrection like his" (Romans 6:3-5).

"O merciful God, grant that the old Adam in these persons may be so buried, that the new man may be raised up in them.

"Grant that all carnal affections may die in them, and that all things belonging to the Spirit may live and grow in them.

"Grant that they may have power and strength, to have victory and to triumph, against the devil, the world, and the flesh.

"Grant that whosoever is here dedicated to thee by our office and ministry may also be endued with heavenly virtues, and everlastingly rewarded, through thy mercy, O blessed Lord God, who dost live, and govern all things, world without end. Amen."

—BAPTISMAL OFFICE, 1662 PRAYER BOOK

Preface

Double vision, like a double exposure in photography, is a displeasing thing. You see two pictures, and that is the trouble, for you ought only to be seeing one, and each of the two that present themselves detracts from the other. The person with double vision sees nothing clearly, and dare not drive a car. The photographer who superimposes one picture on another spoils both.

Something like double vision and double exposure marks much of our thinking about the start of the Christian life. Our minds seem to be split. We talk of *Christian initiation*, meaning admission to the church by baptism, which many of us underwent as infants, and we talk of *becoming a Christian*, referring to the reception of Jesus Christ as Savior and Lord in conversion, which many of us experienced at age. But when we try to relate the two themes, the result is like a doubly-exposed photograph. You can see both pictures, but you cannot make one picture out of them. Each gets in the way of the other, so that neither can be appreciated properly.

Whence comes this split mind? It is the legacy of two centuries of pietism and opposition to pietism. Pietism concentrated on conversion in denominations which were dead or deadish, in which baptism had become an empty formality. Anti-pietists challenged "conversionism" as not appreciating the objectivity of grace in the church's corporate life. To safeguard the importance of conversion, some proponents of infant baptism argued that the regeneration which baptism in some sense mediates is a different thing from the regeneration into which the converted man has come; and some Baptists affirmed that true water-baptism (as opposed to the Spirit-baptism of conversion) is the believer's witness to his response to grace, rather than a sign or means of God's work of grace itself. Thus people have put asunder what God had joined.

The following studies express the view that we cannot think biblically about Christian initiation without focusing on the theme of becoming a Christian, nor vice versa. You only deal as you should with baptism when you concentrate on the Christian's conversion and commitment, on his path and on his prize. The themes of baptism and conversion are not like oil and water, which will not mix, but rather they are like treble and bass in music. You cannot see the full point of either without the other, and you need both to give you proper harmony.

1

The Lord's Command

Baptism is and always was the church's initiation-rite ("Initiation," from a Latin word for "beginning," means reception and entrance into committed membership.) Yes; but what exactly is baptism? And why does it matter?

Baptism is a set action with water and words. By pouring, sprinkling, or immersing, the candidate is momentarily put beneath water, and then brought "out from under." The Greek word *baptizo* means literally "dip," and the action suggests both washing and a new start. The accompanying words—"in the name of the Father, and of the Son, and of the Holy Spirit"—announce a relationship in which the candidate is both claimed by and committed to the Triune God.

Why Baptism?

Pagan religions have washing rituals, and think them important for changing people's inward state. But Christianity says that the inward change which counts before God is a matter of faith—not just correct belief, either, but a living heart-commitment to God through Jesus Christ. This change is not produced by any particular ritual, for it does not depend on any ritual at all. Rituals in emergency are dispensable anyway, and no ritual can help us while we deny or defy God in our hearts. The apostles baptized believers and their dependents, but insisted that what saves is faith—"Believe in the Lord Jesus, and you will be saved" (Acts 16:14ff.; cf. verses 29-33).

But if you can believe and be saved without baptism, why does the church require baptism? Why not give it up, as Quakers and the Salvation Army have done?

The answer appears if we recall basic facts about Jesus, the man from Galilee whom Christians worship as their Savior, Lord, and God.

Jesus Christ

Who was Jesus? Read the Gospels and see! The first three show him as a man who was God, the promised Davidic ruler (Matthew), the suffering servant of prophecy (Mark), and the Spirit-filled evangelist pioneering the path to heaven (Luke), while John presents him as God's only Son, the eternal Word, now made man without loss of deity to bring us life through faith in himself. Next, read the epistles, and watch Paul dwelling on Jesus' divine sonship (Colossians 1:13-20), his redeeming death (Romans 3:21-26; 5:6-11; 2 Corinthians 5:14-21), his rising (1 Corinthians 15:1-20), his present reign (Philippians 2:5-11; 1 Corinthians 15:24-28), and his sure return (1 Thessalonians 4:13—5:11). Watch too how the author of Hebrews blends the themes of Jesus as Son of God and seed of Abraham, apostle and high priest, sacrificer and offering for our sins. Then read how Acts displays Jesus' Lordship as Savior, and how Revelation celebrates his approaching triumph. Put all this together, and you will know who Jesus was.

What is he then to us? Our Master, calling us to serve God by shouldering a cross and following him; our Guide and Friend, who leads and upholds us here and takes us finally to share glory with him hereafter. Lord and lover too, he claims our first loyalty, and if we love him we shall keep his commandments—as indeed he said (John 14:15).

To Please Him

But now our question is answered! For baptism is among Jesus' commands. He sent his followers to disciple all nations, baptizing them in the triune name (Matthew 28:19). So a church that did not require baptism, and an unbaptized Christian who did not ask for it would be something of a contradiction in terms. The root reason for the practice of baptizing is to please Jesus Christ our Lord.

Further Bible Study

The practice of baptizing:
- Acts 8:26-39; 10:30-48

Questions for Thought and Discussion

- What does the Greek word baptizo tell us about the significance of baptism?
- What is the relationship between faith and the ritual act of baptism?
- As a Christian, why should I be baptized?

2

What the Sign Says

There is an autobiography that begins: "I was born (so I am told) ... " That is how I have to speak of my baptism, for I was baptized as a baby. So I expect were many of you. Since the fourth century, if not before (opinions differ), most Christians have been baptized in infancy, and thus have had to take their baptism on trust. If you were baptized in or after your teens, as a first-generation convert or as someone in the Baptist tradition, you will of course remember it vividly. But nothing hangs on that. Baptism, whenever we receive it, belongs now to our past. And we grasp its bearing on today's living not by remembering it as an event, but by understanding it as a speaking sign, a symbol carrying a message; what Augustine calls a visible word from God.

The Message

Whence comes this way of looking at baptism? Why, from Paul, who appeals to baptism to show Christians their calling. In Romans 6:1-14 he says that because we have been buried and raised with Christ in baptism we may not go on in sin. In Colossians 2:8-3:17 he argued that because we have been buried and raised with Christ in baptism we must not lapse into Christless, worldly, "natural" religion, with its legalism and superstition, but must let Christ's supernatural risen life find expression in us in the breaking of bad habits and the hammering out of a new, Christlike character.

Living this way, in conscious solidarity with the living Christ, on a basis of total cancellation of guilt through the cross, is what being a Christian means to Paul, and he sees baptism as signifying the whole of it—both God's work of renewing (our co-crucifixion and co-resurrection with Jesus) and our work of repenting (turning over new leaves to express new life).

Some are puzzled, thinking that Paul, who elsewhere insists that we are justified and saved through faith in Christ, and that alone (Romans 3:27-30; Galatians 2:15ff.; Ephesians 2:8ff.; Philippians 3:4-9), here implies that the baptismal rite as such brings salvation. But this is to misunderstand him, as the following points will show.

(1) Paul writes to first-generation converts whose baptism, according to New Testament custom, would have followed directly on their professing faith; so that believing and being baptized were already linked in their minds as two aspects of the single reality of becoming a Christian.

(2) Assuming this link, Paul reminds them that what they thought of as happening in baptism happened through faith, and not without it. "*In baptism* . . . you were also raised with him [Christ] *through faith*" (Colossians 2:11). Despite popular superstition, sometimes encouraged by clergy who should know better, no Christian tradition—Protestant, Catholic, or Orthodox—allows that baptized persons capable of faith can be saved without faith, or that genuine believers can be lost for being unbaptized.

(3) For Paul and all New Testament writers the link between believing and being baptized is evidently like that between inheriting the throne and being crowned: through the public ceremony the already existing reality of royal privilege is declared, confirmed, celebrated, and formally regularized. (And in the same sense in which Elizabeth II was "*made* queen" at her coronation, the Prayer Book Catechism says that in baptism the believer's child, who is "in the Lord" with his parents from birth, "was *made* a member of Christ, the child of God, and an inheritor of the kingdom of heaven.")

(4) Paul does not in any case invoke baptism as proof of salvation
(baptism alone can never be that; think of Simon the sorcerer
in Acts 8:13-24). He appeals to it, as we said, only as a God-
given sign teaching professed believers what sort of lives they
are called, and committed, and privileged, and enabled to
live.

Live By Your Baptism

When Martin Luther was tempted, as he often was, to doubt God's
love and lapse into the desperate self-indulgence of despair, he
would keep himself steady by telling himself, *"Baptizatus sum
(I have been baptized)."* Thus he recovered assurance that God's
gracious call to him was real, that his new life in Christ was real, and
that he must not falter in his faith or his faithfulness. He had got
the message of baptism! Have we?

Further Bible Study

Baptism picturing salvation:
* Colossians 2:8–3:4
* Romans 6:1-14

Questions for Thought and Discussion

* What does baptism show Christians about themselves?
* What is the relationship between baptism and salvation?
* Why did Martin Luther find reassurance through the fact that he
had been baptized?

3

A Sacrament of Good News

I am awake, after what seems a long sleep. I open my eyes, but all is dark. I realize that I have no idea where I am. I seem to be alone, and whatever is under me is uneven and slippery. Moving will be hazardous, for I can see nothing. Maybe there is nowhere to go; but how can I just stay still? Nothing has meaning. Hopelessness makes me feel sick—small, weak, and scared. But I think I hear a voice in the distance: "come, there is light here." I cannot locate the voice with certainty as yet, but I know that the only thing for me is to try to grope towards it as best I can.

Voice in the Dark

The adult convert has been described as a phenomenon of our times, and many adults now Christians began their pilgrimage in a state of mind describable in these terms. No wonder! For the starting-point of Bible Christianity is precisely a voice in the dark, a call from God to the benighted, a word which is not truly heard, familiar though its theme may be, till one knows that one is spiritually in the dark, alone and lost. It is by inducing this knowledge that the Holy Spirit enables adults to hear what God is saying.

"Word of God" is a description belonging to both Jesus Christ and the Bible, since both reveal God's mind; but "word of God" in the New Testament usually denotes the gospel—that is, the good news (which is what "gospel" means) concerning God's love to the lost. This is the word which God himself speaks into the dark chaos of our consciousness.

Out of Darkness

What does God say in the gospel? He announces the most staggering free gift of all time. He offers total rescue (that is, *salvation*) from the rebellious nonconformity to himself which is the root of all our guilt, misery, and frustration, and whose Bible name is *sin*. He promises a new, endless life of pardon, peace, moral power, and joyful purpose to all who are humble enough not to try and earn it, but simply to receive it.

How can God make this offer? Through Christ's death as a sacrifice for sins. How do we receive this life? By renouncing rebellion, and embracing the risen Savior as our Master; the life is found within that relationship. What happens then? Increasingly we prove the truth of Jesus' words, "He who follows me will not walk in darkness, but will have the light of life" (John 8:12).

Reflected Glory

Many today see baptism as an ecclesiastical formality, significant only for naming a child, and some Christians, dreading ideas of regenerative magic, deliberately play baptism down; but the church Fathers celebrated it as something wonderful and precious. When they extolled baptism as the gate of life, were they carrying over the pagan notion that rituals correctly performed harness supernatural powers? No—though their language has often been taken this way. But they were really celebrating the magnificent meaning of baptism, as guaranteeing to the believer fulfillment of the magnificent gospel promise of salvation. The glory of baptism was to them, as it should be to us, the reflected glory of the gospel.

Confirming solemn promises by visible, tangible tokens—documents signed and sealed, gifts, handshakes, shared meals or drinks—is the most natural thing in the world, and if what is promised is exciting, receiving and possessing the token will bring delight. Ask a happily married woman what thoughts a glance at her wedding ring triggers off! So, too, baptism expresses a lover's commitment—God's!—guaranteeing endless happiness, and receiving and reflecting on baptism is meant to bring us joy.

For it was the Savior himself who, to confirm the promise of salvation, instituted the two gospel sacraments, baptism and the Supper. The Eastern church called them "mysteries," meaning disclosures of what was previously hidden (the word was used for initiation into cults). The Western church called them "sacraments," meaning solemn pledges (the word was used for the Roman soldier's oath of loyalty). Nowadays Baptists and many evangelicals call them "ordinances," because Christ commanded the church to observe them. Both baptism and the Lord's Supper are visual aids to understanding and visible incentives to trusting, and both need to be viewed in both these ways if their true glory is to be seen.

Do you see it now?

Further Bible Study

God confirming his promises:
- the covenant, confirmed by circumcision—Genesis 17
- the hope of glory, confirmed by oath—Hebrews 6:11-20
- forgiveness of sins, confirmed by the cup—Matthew 26:20-29

Questions for Thought and Discussion

- Why are both the Bible and Jesus Christ referred to as the "Word of God"?
- What does it mean to say that "the glory of baptism was . . . the reflected glory of the gospel"?
- What did the Eastern church mean by "mysteries" and the Western church by "sacraments," and what do both words tell us about baptism?

4

Conversion and Baptism

"Convert" means "change." "We were converted last year," a lady told me—she meant that her home was now on North Sea gas. And the van with "Conversions Our Specialty" on it belongs to a coachbuilder (not an evangelist!). But our subject now is Christian conversion, the vital inner change whereby we turn, or rather are turned (for conversion is God's work in us), so that we live with, in, through, and for God henceforth.

What is Conversion?

Luke writes of this in Acts, where Christ sends Paul to the Gentiles "to *open their eyes*, that they may *turn* (convert) . . . from the power of Satan *to God*, that they may receive *forgiveness of sins* and a place among those who are sanctified (made acceptable) *by faith* in me" (26:18). Paul summons Gentiles to "*repent and turn* (convert) *to God*" (26:20), and God opens "a *door of faith*" (14:27) to them, resulting in "the *conversion* of the Gentiles" (15:3). We see close-ups of conversion in the stories of Paul himself, who for all his religiosity had no vital link with God till Christ found him (9:1-30); of the Ethiopian eunuch (8:27-39); of Cornelius the God-fearer (10:22-

48); and of the Philippian jailer (16:27-34); to whom we might add the anonymous prostitute and Zacchaeus the extortioner in Luke's Gospel (7:36-50; 19:1-10).

Conversion, we see, means commitment to God in response to mercy from God, and consists of repentance and faith. In Scripture these two overlap. Repentance is not just regretful remorse, but a total about-turn in one's thoughts, aims, and acts, so that one leaves the paths of self-willed disobedience to serve God in faith and faithfulness. Faith is not just believing Christian truth, but forsaking self-confidence and man-made hopes to trust wholly in Christ and his cross for pardon, peace, and life, so that henceforth one lives to one's lover-God in thankful, penitent obedience.

Though before conversion God may work in one's life in obvious ways, making one seek him as Paul and Augustine did and inducing what Wesley called "the faith of a servant," only by conversion does one become a Christian in the full scriptural sense, exercising "the faith of a son." Spiritually, till conversion all is twilight at best.

Conversion is sometimes dismissed as a uniquely evangelical phenomenon, but it belongs to mainstream Christian experience everywhere. It need not be dramatically sudden or emotional, nor does one have to be fully aware of what is happening (though a conscious conversion usually proves a blessing). What is crucial, however, is that the marks of conversion—faith and repentance as principles of daily living—should be found in us; otherwise, we cannot be judged Christians at all, whatever experiences we may claim. Thus, the converted life-style is more significant than any conversion experience.

Where Baptism Comes In

Fine, you say, but what has this to do with baptism? You can, of course, be converted without knowing about baptism, just as you can be baptized and know nothing of conversion. For all that, however, there is a threefold connection.

First, baptism *requires* conversion. It signifies not only God's saving work in us, through Jesus' death and resurrection for us, but also our entry thereby into the new life through "repentance to God and . . . faith in our Lord Jesus Christ" (Acts 20:21)—that is, through conversion. Conversion, credibly professed, qualifies adults for baptism, and it is to conversion that baptism commits infants.

Second, baptism *shapes* conversion. From the symbolism of baptism we learn that becoming a Christian means accepting death with Christ (entire separation from the world), being washed through Christ (entire forgiveness for the past), and identifying with the risen life of Christ (entire consecration for the future); and that genuine conversion has to be a real response to God at all three points.

Third, baptism *tests* conversion. Conversion as a psychological recoil to religion is known outside Christianity; what identifies a conversion experience as Christian is its positive orientation to baptism's threefold summons.

What, I wonder, does your baptism say about the Christian commitment, or conversion, that you profess? You will be wise to check and see.

Further Bible Study

True conversion:
- 1 Thessalonians 1; 2:9-16

Questions for Thought and Discussion

- Who does the work of Christian conversion, and what is that work?
- "Only by conversion does one become a Christian in the full scriptural sense." Why?
- Why is a converted life-style more significant than a conversion experience?

5

Baptized in Jesus' Name

When Peter, preaching at Pentecost, told the Jews that the man they murdered was risen and reigning, many were flabbergasted and asked what they ought to do. "Repent," said Peter, "and be baptized every one of you in the name of Jesus Christ for the forgiveness of your sins" (Acts 2:38). It is easy to miss the full force of this. Peter was prescribing not a formal gesture of regret for the crucifixion, but total renunciation of independence as a way of living and total submission to the rule of the risen Lord. For Jesus' name carries Jesus' claim, and undergoing baptism is, for those who have reached years of discretion, a sign that the claim is being accepted.

Name and Claim

Paul shows this when he says that at the Exodus the Israelites "all were baptized into Moses"—that is, as the NEB paraphrases, "received baptism into the fellowship of Moses"—by obediently following their God-sent leader where the cloud led, through the divided sea (1 Corinthians 10:1ff). Paul shows it more clearly still when he reminds his converts that they do not owe him exclusive loyalty, nor should they fight for his honor, since they were not "baptized in the name of Paul" (1 Corinthians 1:13). The implication is that baptism to Paul was, among other things, an enlistment ceremony, publicly transacting a pledge of loyalty whereby one undertakes to be, as the Prayer Book puts it, "Christ's faithful soldier and servant" for life.

What does this pledge involve? The Bible idea which makes it clearest is Jesus' own picture in John 10 of himself as shepherd, and his followers as his flock. The good shepherd, says Jesus, precedes, pastures, and protects his sheep (verses 4, 9 11ff.), and following where he leads is the whole of the sheep's task (verse 3ff.).

A recurring New Testament theme is of Jesus as pioneer, blazing the trail to glory for us—which is the good shepherd leading the sheep home.

Again, a classical way of viewing Jesus' ministry is in terms of the three anointed offices of the Old Testament: prophet, priest, and king. As prophet, whose teaching about God is wholly from God, Jesus is the good shepherd guiding, by showing the way to life. (For Jesus' teaching, read the Gospels.) As priest, set between us and God to secure our joy of fellowship with God, sacrificing himself for our sins and now helping us from heaven, Jesus is the good shepherd saving the sheep at the cost of his life (John 10:11, 15, 17ff.; for Jesus' priesthood, read Hebrews). Then as king, lord of our circumstances, consciences, and conduct, Jesus is the good shepherd keeping his sheep from evil of all kinds. (For Jesus' kingdom, read Revelation.)

So everyone baptized in Jesus' name must become Jesus' follower. He must *attend* to Jesus as God's messenger—"This is my beloved Son . . . listen to him" (Matthew 17:5). He must *trust* in Jesus as God's mediator—"Come to me . . . and I will give you rest" (Matthew 11:28). And he must obey Jesus as his Master—"Why do you call me 'Lord, Lord,' and not do what I tell you?" (Luke 6:46). You and I were baptized; do we live thus?

The New Society

Nor is this all. By acknowledging Jesus as our shepherd we affirm identification with his flock—the community for which "Jesus people" is the perfect name, the Christian church. They are our *compatriots,* fellow-nationals, for "we . . . are citizens of heaven" (Philippians 3:20, NEB); they are our *brothers,* with us in God's family, for "you are all brethren" (Matthew 23:8); and they are *limbs* with us in the ministering organism which is Christ's body, for "all of us are the parts of one body" (Ephesians 4:25, NEB) and "you are all one person in Christ Jesus" (Galatians 3:28, NEB).

So baptism has social implications. Involvement in the "body life" of mutual sympathy and service for Christ must be the rule for all the baptized. (See, on this, Romans 12:4ff.; 1 Corinthians 12:4ff.; Ephesians 4:7-16; 1 Peter 4:10ff.). Isolationism in church—sitting apart, not getting acquainted, dodging responsibility and so on—is often condemned as denying the meaning of the Lord's Supper; we need to see that it denies the meaning of baptism too, and just as drastically. Is that clear to us now? And are we making it a matter of conscience that by active love of our fellow-Christians we should show that we know what our baptism means?

Further Bible Study

What Jesus asks of disciples:
- Luke 9:57-62; 14:25-33
- John 13:1-17

Questions for Thought and Discussion

- In what way is baptism the end of one way of life and the beginning of another?
- Why may we rightly refer to baptism as an enlistment ceremony?
- What does baptism have to do with "body life"?

6

Washing

When you look at the two gospel sacraments (or ordinances, as some prefer to say) which Jesus left us, you realize that they are just slices of ordinary home life—a meal, with a wash preceding. Jesus' choice of these two everyday events to be signs of saving grace shows us that as without washing and eating our physical health suffers, so without their evangelical counterparts spiritual health is not found.

Cleansing from Sin

What is the evangelical counterpart of washing? Being cleansed from the guilt and filth of sin. Without this "heavenly washing,"[1] our holy Creator will not accept us. Like parents who will not have their children at the table till they have washed their hands, God will not have us at his table—that is, in his fellowship—till our dirt is off.

We have to realize that the arrogance, selfishness, meanness, and sheer perversity of our unloving and unlovely lives is to God something impure, offensive, and repellent, and he recoils from it as we do when we are faced with dirt where we had a right to expect cleanliness. If in a restaurant you were offered food on a plate that had obviously not been washed, you would feel disgusted and decline to accept it. Similarly, according to Scripture, our Maker's attitude to persons dominated by the anti-law, anti-God syndrome called sin is one of resolute rejection, "wrath," to be shown forth in "righteous judgment" when the day comes.

"The wrath of God," says Paul, "is revealed from heaven against all ungodliness and wickedness of men." "God's decree [is] that those who do such things deserve to die." "When God's righteous judgment will be revealed . . . he will render to every man according to his works . . . there will be tribulation and distress for every human being who does evil" (Romans 1:18, 32; 2:5ff., 9).

The first thing that Jesus' prescription of baptism for all disciples (Matthew 28:19) shows us is that we all need "heavenly washing." Baptism is a standing witness against any playing down of this need by querying whether God takes note of our guilt and uncleanness, or whether his wrath is "for real." But it shows more! Baptism shows that "heavenly washing" can be real for all.

Blood, Faith, Baptism

This washing is momentous. It includes both the canceling of guilt by pardon and the breaking of sin's dominion—that is, our enslavement to motives which, by exalting and indulging self, defile and pollute our whole lives. What cures this bondage is inward renewal, that is, regeneration, of which more later.

How can this washing be? "The blood of Jesus his Son cleanses us from all sin" (1 John 1:7). Well did Toplady pray that Jesus' sacrificial death would *Be of sin the double cure,/Cleanse me from its guilt and power.*" Christ's blood (that is, the power of his death) will "purify your conscience from dead [that is, guilty and therefore death-dealing] works to serve the living God" (through sin's reign over you being broken) (Hebrews 9:14). "If I do not wash you," said Jesus to Peter, speaking of this inner cleansing, though Peter missed the reference, "you are not in fellowship with me" (John 13:8, NEB).

When are we thus washed? When we believe—that is, commit ourselves to Christ. What then has baptism to do with it? Three things. First, baptism symbolically *pictures* it, for our learning, as we saw. Second, baptism visibly *promises* it, proclaiming that whoever has faith in Christ will receive it. Third, baptism formally *presents* it, and so assures the believing recipient that he really has it, just as presenting the hood at graduation assures the student that he really has secured his degree. It is in these terms—picture, promise, and presentation—that we should understand Peter calling Jews to baptism "for the forgiveness of your sins" (Acts 2:38), and later defining baptism " . . . not as a removal of dirt from the body but as an appeal to God for a clear conscience" (1 Peter 3:21), and Ananias urging Paul, "Rise and be baptized, and wash away your sins, calling on (Jesus') name" (Acts 22:16).

"You were washed," said Paul to the Corinthians (1 Corinthians 6:11). Are you washed, as they were? Like me, you need to be.

Note:
[1]*The 1662 Prayer Book*

Further Bible Study

Cleansing from sin's uncleanness:
- pictured, 2 Kings 5:1-14
- promised, Ezekiel 36:22-32
- realized, Titus 2:11-3:8

Questions for Thought and Discussion

- How is sin described in this chapter? What does this mean?
- Why do we need more than pardon alone?
- Why can we not have fellowship with Christ without being spiritually washed?

7

United with Christ

Is there more to Christianity than practicing morality and supporting a church? Many think not, but there is. Christianity is a new life, consisting of new relationships with God, men, and things; and it all springs from one source—a unique link between the Christian and his Master, Jesus Christ.

The New Testament makes this quite clear, but talks of the link itself in language that is startling and hard to pin down. Union with Christ is affirmed in terms that sound too strong to be true. Thus, Paul says that "Christ . . . is our life" (Colossians 3:4), and "I live; yet not I, but Christ liveth in me" (Galatians 2:20 KJV); and he speaks of Christians doing and experiencing literally everything in Christ, and of baptized persons as having put on Christ (Galatians 3:27). So, too, Jesus says, "Abide in me, and I in you . . . I am the vine, you are the branches" (John 15:4ff.). What sort of link can it be that prompts such statements?

Twofold Union

The link has two aspects. Take them separately.

First, it is a relation to *Jesus' person*—one of *discipleship*. The Jesus of the Gospels is alive today, risen and real. In terms of character, attitudes, and concerns, he remains just what he was in his earthly life—"Jesus Christ is the same yesterday and today and for ever"

(Hebrews 13:8). And he calls us to do just what he called his first disciples to do—give him total loyalty and love, learn from him, and faithfully obey him, denying ourselves in order to identify with his will at all points, so that what he is finds its reflection in what we are. This is the new commitment aspect of our link with Jesus.

Second, this link is also a relation to what theologians sometimes call the *Christ-event*. The usual label for it is *incorporation*. We should understand this aspect of the union as follows.

God's eternal Son became Jesus the Christ by incarnation; to put away our sins he tasted death by crucifixion; he resumed bodily life for all eternity by resurrection; and he reentered heaven's glory by ascension. This is the Christ-event. It is truly historical, for it happened in Palestine 2,000 years ago. Equally true, however, it is transhistorical, in the sense of not being bounded by space and time as other events are: it can touch and involve in itself any person at any time anywhere. Faith in Jesus occasions that involving touch, so that in terms of rock-bottom reality every believer has actually died and risen, and now lives and reigns, with Jesus and through Jesus. (Note that when the phrase "in Christ" is used, "in" is shorthand for "with" and "through" together.) This is the new creation aspect of our link with Jesus.

We have looked at the two aspects separately so as to get clear about each, as a pianist learning a piece might do with first the right-hand, then the left-hand notes. But as both sets of notes must be played together to produce the proper sound, so we must mentally fuse both aspects of our link with Jesus if we are to affirm it scripturally. The way to express it is that in the Jesus to whom we go in faith the power of the whole Christ-event resides, and that in saving us he not only sets us right with God, but also, so to speak, plugs us in to his own dying, rising, and reigning. Thus we live in joyful fellowship with him, knowing ourselves justified by faith through his death, and finding therewith freedom from sin's tyranny and foretastes of heaven on earth through the transforming power within us that his dying and rising exerts.

This is an over-short statement of an overwhelming truth. The classic expositions of it are Romans 6-8 and Colossians 3: both should be studied.

Baptism and Union

Baptism bears directly on all this; for by taking the candidate momentarily under water, baptism signifies not only the washing away of sin's guilt but also the dying and rising with Christ that brings freedom from sin's rule. "Have you forgotten," writes Paul, "that when we were baptized into union with Christ Jesus we were baptized into his death? By baptism we were buried with him, and lay dead, in order that, as Christ was raised from the dead in the splendour of the Father, so also we might set our feet upon the new path of life" (Romans 6:3ff., NEB).

If anyone wants to know the real nature and heart of Christianity, let him look at baptism; for baptism proclaims in both aspects together the link with the living Lord that makes all things new.

Further Bible Study

Life in the Son:
- John 6:35-59; 16:1-11
- 2 Corinthians 5:14-21
- Galatians 3:23-29

Questions for Thought and Discussion

- Is Christianity primarily a matter of morality or of relationship? Explain your answer.
- What does the fact that Jesus Christ never changes tell us about discipleship?
- What is meant by saying that the Christ-event is transhistorical? What does this fact imply for you?

8

Baptism and the Holy Spirit

Before Jesus' public ministry began, John the Baptist contrasted his water-baptism with the Spirit-baptism which the Coming One would administer. "I have baptized you with water; but he will baptize you with the Holy Spirit" (Mark 1:8). Before his ascension, looking on to Pentecost, Jesus drew the same contrast: "John baptized with water, but before many days you shall be baptized with the Holy Spirit" (Acts 1:5).

The point was not that Spirit-baptism and water-baptism are opposed, or that Spirit-baptism makes water-baptism needless, but that John's baptism belonged to the last days of the old covenant, whereas Christ's outpouring of the Spirit (cf. Acts 2:33) would initiate believers into the life of the new covenant as predicted in Jeremiah 31:31ff., proclaimed by Jesus at the Supper (1 Corinthians 11:25), and presented in detail in Hebrews 8:8-10:25.

New Covenant Gift

What is new covenant life? It is a realizing of fellowship with Jesus Christ in his glory, and with his Father as our Father through him, plus a realized sharing in the benefits of his atoning death (pardon, peace, acceptance, adoption) and of his risen life (present help, lasting hope). To give this life is the Spirit's distinctive post-Pentecostal ministry.

That is why in John 7:39 the apostle notes that the Spirit, the agent of creation (Genesis 1:2), the inspirer of prophecy (2 Peter 1:21), and the enabler of Jesus himself (Luke 3:22; 4:14, 18), "as yet . . . had not been given [literally, was not yet,] because Jesus was not yet glorified." The Spirit was fulfilling other functions all along, but he could only start making known in men's hearts Jesus' glory as the crucified and risen Lord after Jesus' death and resurrection had actually happened.

When New Testament writers speak of folk *receiving* the Spirit, what they have in mind is initiation into the new covenant experience, with the bold, joyful, exuberant self-expression in praise and witness (sometimes, indeed, tongues and prophecy, whatever these were) that the experience brings. (See Acts 2:38; 8:15; 10:47; 19:2; Romans 8:15; Galatians 3:2.) In this sense, the Old Testament believers, who antedated Christ, did not receive the Spirit. But since all repentance and response to what one knows of God's mercy is Spirit-taught and Spirit-wrought, we must insist that in another, more basic sense, they did, as did the Samaritans before Peter and John arrived—despite Acts 8:15ff!

Springing from new covenant experience, New Testament language about the Spirit naturally focuses on this experience, and does not always have the more basic point in view—though the writers are quite clear that repentance and faith, where found, are God's gift (Acts 5:31; 11:18; Ephesians 2:8).

What then is "baptism in the Spirit"? Following Jesus in Acts 1:5, we define it as the Spirit's coming to someone to begin in him the new covenant ministry as described. For Jesus' disciples, this happened at Pentecost, though they had faith before; to all others it happens at conversion. For any post-conversion experience today, "baptism in the Spirit" is a misnomer.

Christian Initiation

Since Pentecost, becoming a member of God's family according to his revealed will—Christian initiation, to use the technical phrase—has involved three factors: repentance and faith, plus Christian baptism, plus the coming of the Spirit for new covenant ministry (cf. Acts 2:38; Romans 8:9ff.; Ephesians 1:13ff.). In experience, the order has varied; apparently it was faith-baptism-Spirit at Pentecost (Acts 2:38-42), Spirit-faith-baptism at the "Gentile Pentecost" (10:44-48), faith-Spirit-baptism at Galatia (Galatians 3:2); certainly, it has been baptism-faith-Spirit for all those Christians down the centuries who were baptized as infants. The order scarcely matters; what matters is that all three links between us and Jesus Christ— faith, baptism, Spirit—should actually be there.

When Paul says that in the one *Spirit* we were all *baptized* (that is, by Christ) into his one *body* (1 Corinthians 12:13), he thinks of water-baptism and the gift of the Spirit as two complementary aspects of a single act of Christ, who claims and incorporates or engrafts us (Paul's image, Romans 11:17-24) into vital union with himself. So converts who have received the Spirit should seek baptism, and the baptized should seek conversion, so that they may receive the Spirit! In God's revealed purpose for our lives, water-baptism and Spirit-baptism are joined. Let not any of us in thought or practice put them asunder.

Further Bible Study

Filled with the Spirit:
- Acts 6:1-10
- Ephesians 5:15-20

The Spirit in the body:
- 1 Corinthians 12:1-13

Questions for Thought and Discussion

- What is the new covenant? Do you believe yourself to be personally included in the new covenant? Why?
- In what sense did Old Testament believers not receive the Spirit? In what sense did they receive him?
- What is Spirit-baptism? What does it have to do with the body of Christ?

9

Basic Christianity

Being a Christian is a blend of doctrine, experience, and practice. Head, heart, and legs are all involved. Doctrine and experience without practice would turn me into a knowledgeable spiritual paralytic; experience and practice without doctrine would leave me a restless spiritual sleepwalker. If Christ is to be formed in me, doctrine, experience, and practice must all be there together.

Now Christianity holds that the Creator is known through material realities—the natural order, Jesus' flesh, and prescribed symbols, of which baptism is one. Often, and easily, Christianity is distorted and misunderstood: ask six people to define it, and you will probably get six divergent answers. But baptism, as instituted by Jesus, is a standing witness to what essential doctrine, experience, and practice really are.

Trinity

The doctrine baptism displays is *the Triune God in covenant with man.* Jesus prescribed baptism "in the name of the Father and of the Son and of the Holy Spirit" (Matthew 28:19). "Name" means, as often in Scripture, "personal being," and is singular, pointing to the fact that the three persons are, by mysterious essential unity, not three

Gods but one. "In" (literally, "towards") points to a relationship established between each of the three and ourselves.

As the Trinity is the most startling, difficult, and distinctive doctrine of Christianity, setting it wholly apart from all other forms of faith in God, so it is the most basic truth of Christianity, for the whole gospel rests upon it. According to Scripture, it is the cooperation of the three that brings salvation. Let us spell this out.

The Father planned to save, choosing his Son to be our sacrifice (1 Peter 1:20) and us sinners to be his people (Ephesians 1:4); now he is carrying his plan through. The Son at his Father's will took flesh and redeemed us, paying on the cross the price of our sins (1 John 4:9ff.) and overcoming death forever by his resurrection; now he lives to intercede for his own (Romans 8:27; Hebrews 7:25)—that is, to act on their behalf so that they gain all he won for them. The Spirit, sent by the Father and the Son (John 14:26; 15:26), re-creates us by new birth (John 3:5ff.; 2 Corinthians 5:17), leads us to know Christ by faith (Ephesians 1:17ff.; 3:16ff.), and changes us into Christ's likeness (2 Corinthians 3:18).

Deny the personal deity of the Son or Spirit, and you call in question that person's ministry; and then salvation falls to the ground. So Christ's baptismal formula, affirming the tri-unity of the God to whom we are dedicated, safeguards the gospel in a fundamental way.

Justification

The experience baptism depicts is *leaving defilement behind*: having one's guilty failures washed out, so that one can start again. The double symbolism of washing and resurrection proclaims this. Thus baptism expresses the gospel message of God's sustained forgiveness and acceptance of us as we trust in Jesus' shed blood—the message, that is, of justification by faith (Paul's phrase: see Romans 3:21-5:21; Galatians 2:15-3:29).

Moral failure is a universal fact, and guilt, shame, and a defiled and accusing conscience are the commonest human experiences. So the cleansing of conscience, not just once but daily, is a universal need, and the experience which baptism symbolizes is one without which anyone who knows himself at all well can hardly live. "Foul, I to the fountain fly; Wash me, Savior, or I die."

Repentance

The path of practice to which baptism directs is *consenting to be changed*, which is the essence of repentance. I do not baptize myself; the minister is in charge, putting me under the water and bringing me out at his own will. This pictures true penitence and self-denial, that is, surrendering to Christ the reins of one's life, so as to be driven his way. Self-assertion and stubbornness come naturally to everyone, and W. H. Auden's line, "We would rather be ruined than changed," is too true to be good. But willingness to be changed by Christ (which is not a natural state of mind, but a gift of grace) remains the fundamental element in all genuine Christian practice.

Baptism requires us to face, and keep facing, these basic norms of doctrine, experience, and practice in Christ's Christianity. This in itself is a major part of the blessing baptism brings.

Further Bible Study

Doctrine, experience, practice:
- Romans 6:15-7:6

Questions for Thought and Discussion

- What does baptism have to do with the doctrine of the Trinity?
- What double symbolism do we see in baptism, and what does it say about us?
- How does baptism challenge the statement "We would rather be ruined than changed"?

10

Baptism and Infants

One of the church's unhappy divisions concerns the subject of baptism.

Nobody defends baptizing all infants as such, but most denominations baptize the children of the baptized. Baptists, however, see this as either non-baptism (because infants cannot make the required confession of faith) or as irregular baptism (because, they say, it is not clearly apostolic, nor pastorally wise). Some hold that by not actually commanding infant baptism God in Scripture forbids it; all urge that to postpone baptism till faith is conscious is always in practice best. (Note that when I speak of "Baptists" here, I am referring to a whole range of Christians—members of Baptist and baptistic denominations, along with some charismatics, independents, and other evangelicals—for whom believer-baptism is the standard practice.)

On the other side, some have deduced from covenant theology that God commands the baptism of believers' babies after all. Many more maintain that this practice, though fixed by the church, has better theological, historical, and pastoral warrant than the alternative has, and so should be thought of as "most agreeable with the institution of Christ."[1]

How should we view the issue? Weigh these points.

Over-Arguing

First: many on both sides of the question seem to over-argue. Scripture neither commands nor forbids infant baptism, and we may not assume that the divine Author who guided the human writers meant to do either.

Male infant circumcision by God's command under the old covenant, linked with Paul's insistence that under the new covenant a believer's children are "holy" (dedicated to God and accepted by him) along with their parent(s) (see Genesis 17:9-14; 1 Corinthians 7:14), make infant baptism look right to many Bible-believing Christians. If parent-and-child solidarity under God's covenant is an unchanging fact, on which was based God's former command of circumcision (the then covenant sign for baby boys), how can it be proper to deny baptism (the new covenant sign) to babies now?

Moreover, infant baptism was pretty certainly apostolic practice. The "houses" (that is, households, which were extended families) of Lydia, the Philippian jailer, and Stephanas were baptized, the second within hours of the jailer's conversion (Acts 16:15, 33; 1 Corinthians 1:16). It seems only natural to infer that this was standard practice when any head of a home was converted, and that these extended families contained infants. Luke and Paul would hardly have said "house" without qualification if they had meant us to gather that on principle babies were excluded.

It must be conceded that theological propriety and apparent precedent, though surely justifying infant baptism today, add up to less than a divine command.

At the same time, however, arguments against infant baptism cannot be made conclusively. For example:

(1) It is urged that a confession of faith is part of the definition of baptism. But the New Testament nowhere says that; it is a question-begging inference from the fact that in the New Testament, as in later practice, adults are not baptized without such a confession.

(2) It is urged that baptized infants will never be required to confess personal faith at all. But parents and godparents sponsoring infants at baptism commit those infants to genuine personal repentance and faith, compelling them to make their own genuine confession of repentance and faith at age,

and in confirmation and all equivalent rites of reception into adult church membership, the requirement of personal confession is central. In other words, infant baptism demands adult conversion.

(3) It is urged that infant baptism prompts presumption, being thought to regenerate and save without need for faith. Baptists shake their heads over the Anglican Prayer Book's declaration after baptism, "Seeing now this child is regenerate," and the statement in the Catechism that "in my baptism ... I was made a member of Christ, the child of God, and an inheritor of the kingdom of heaven." But these phrases denote only the ceremonial making over to us of spiritual rights and privileges, which if it is ever to be effectual must be confirmed by faith in Christ. As Archbishop Usher wrote long ago, I only "have the profit and benefit of them (these promises of grace), when I come to understand what grant God in Baptism hath sealed unto me, and actually lay hold on it by faith."

Pastoral

Baptists, anxious to express the God-taught concept of the church as believers only, dedicate infants (a "dry baptism," from the infant-baptist standpoint) and baptize with water at age. Other Protestants, anxious also to express the Biblical solidarity of the family in the covenant, baptize infants and confirm at age (a "dry baptism," from the Baptist standpoint). For infant-baptist and adult-baptist groups to work together in mutual respect should never be hard, because biblically and pastorally the two practices are (thank God!) parallel in their meaning.

Note:

[1]*Anglican Article XXVII*

Further Bible Study

God's grace in children:
- 1 Samuel 3
- Luke 2:5-25
- Ephesians 6:1-4

Questions for Thought and Discussion

- What similarities are noted between circumcision and baptism? How far do they justify infant baptism? How would you argue your view against those who judge differently?
- What should be required of adults being baptized that cannot be expected of infants?
- Will baptized babies necessarily receive the spiritual benefits symbolized by the rite? Why or why not?

11

Baptism, Confirmation, Confession

Most of the historic denominations admit folk baptized as infants to Holy Communion by means of a confirmation rite. Typically the pastor or the bishop lays hands on the candidates and prays that the Holy Spirit will strengthen them. What does this mean?

A False Trail

First of all, it does not mean that thus far the indwelling Spirit's personal presence, or gifts, or some aspects of his regenerating, sanctifying, and assuring ministry have been in some way withheld. Nor does it mean that through confirmation we receive the Spirit and his benefits in ways that otherwise could not be. Such ideas are common, but they are really superstitions, reflecting medieval belief that confirmation is a sacrament, which Peter and John were administering when they laid hands on the Samaritans after praying for the Spirit (Acts 8:14-17), and that sacraments are ordinarily the only means of conveying the blessings they signify.

But none of this is right. The New Testament knows only two sacraments (or ordinances, as Baptists would say), in the sense of

God-given signs guaranteeing particular blessings to believers; namely, baptism and the Lord's Supper. The gesture of laying hands on the person you pray for as a mark of goodwill and concern, as did Peter and John to the Samaritans, and Paul to the Ephesian disciples, and the Antioch leaders to Paul and Barnabas (Acts 19:6; 13:4), and Paul and an unidentified eldership to Timothy (2 Timothy 1:6; 1 Timothy 4:14), is a different thing.

Also, Scripture shows that the grace-gifts signified and guaranteed to believers by the sacraments may be given them apart from the sacraments. Remission of sins, which is one part of justification, is an obvious example: compare Acts 2:38, 22:16 with Romans 3:21-5:1 and Galatians 3.

Certainly, the New Testament idea of initiation is of becoming a Christian-in-the-church. There is no "flight of the alone to the Alone"; we are saved in company, as units in the body of Christ, or not at all. Certainly, too, scriptural initiation involves faith, exercised and professed; reception into the believing community by baptism in the triune name; and receiving, or being sealed with, the gift of the Holy Spirit (Acts 2:38; 2 Corinthians 1:22; 5:5; Ephesians 1:13ff.; 4:30). But it is not true, as some have supposed, that confirmation supplements baptism by signifying the gift of the Spirit. In the New Testament baptism signifies all aspects of entering new life in Christ, including the gift of the Spirit (Acts 2:38; 1 Corinthians 12:13). Confirmation, however, is no part of scriptural initiation, for it is not a biblical ordinance at all.

"I Do"

But if it is just church tradition, why practice it? Is it worth retaining? Yes, for two reasons, one theological, one pastoral.

First: there is one element in Christian initiation for which infant baptism does not provide; namely, personal confession of faith before the church. We may regard the baptism of believers' babies as God's will, but confession of faith when old enough is equally God's will (Baptists are right there!—see Romans 10:9; 1 Corinthians 12:3; 1 Timothy 6:12). Personal confession shows that we can "discern the body"—that is, see the meaning and relevance for ourselves of Jesus' words at the Last Supper, "This is my body which is for you" (1 Corinthians 11:29, 24). Personal confession thus qualifies us for welcome at Holy Communion, which is for believers only. Confirmation confirms fitness to share this central act of worship.

Second: confirmation is the point in Christian nurture where junior, sponsored church membership is exchanged for adult membership in our own right, based on personal acceptance of the commitment to faith and renunciation of the devil, the world, and the flesh which the infants' sponsors made on their behalf. In the Anglican Prayer Book service, for example, the bishop asks: "Do you here, in the presence of God, and of this Congregation, renew the solemn promise and vow made in your name at your Baptism; ratifying and confirming the same in your own persons?" The prescribed reply is "I do"—which, if sincerely uttered, here as in the marriage service speaks volumes. Then the church, having heard the candidates confirm their faith by confessing it, prays with the bishop that all may be confirmed—established and strengthened—by God's Spirit for the fulfilling of their commitment.

Edifying? Good Christian sense? What do you think?

When taken seriously, confirmation becomes a profound occasion of commitment or recommitment, and of witness to the saving work of Christ embraced by faith.

Further Bible Study

The committed confessor:
- 1 Timothy 6:11-21
- 2 Timothy 1:8-14

Questions for Thought and Discussion

- Why is it important to recognize that God's grace-gifts do not come to us only through the sacraments?
- What is the importance of personal confession?
- Why is Holy Communion for believers only?

12

Baptism and Body Life

What is a Christian? Baptism tells us: not a mere do-gooder, but someone converted and committed to the living Christ, a born-again person washed from his sins through Christ's blood and now indwelt by Christ's Spirit. What is the church? Again, baptism tells us: not a mere club, an organized interest group, but a supernatural organism of believers so linked to their Master, and through him to each other, that all are truly "members"—that is, "limbs," "working parts"—of one "body" of which he is "Head." As there is one body, one Lord, and one faith, says Paul, so there is one baptism (Ephesians 4:4ff.); one, because union by faith with the Lord in that one body is what baptism always signifies.

By "church member" we normally mean one who has been received into a worshipping community; by "body of Christians" we usually mean a denomination. But the New Testament knows neither church members nor Christian bodies, only members of Christ, and of his body. Our usage stemmed from Scripture, but has parted company with both the Bible's grammar and its meaning. In scripture, Christ's body is essentially ordinary folk living together a new and extraordinary life because the risen Lord has touched and claimed and now controls them. When we say "body" or "member," this should be the thought in our minds.

Ethics of the Body

"Body life" is a current term for the network of mutual relationships which Christ both calls and causes the limbs of his body to build. As a sign of incorporation into "the mystical body of (God's) Son, which is the blessed company of all faithful people,"[1] baptism commits us not only to personal conversion, but also, with that, to practicing the ethics of body life in the Christian family. Scripture spells out these ethics in terms of first valuation and then service.

(1) *Valuation.* "All baptized in Christ, you have all clothed yourselves in Christ, and there are no more distinctions between Jew and Greek, slave and free, male and female, but all of you are one in Christ Jesus" (Galatians 3:27ff., JB). The racial, social, economic, cultural, and sexual distinctions which operate as restraints on our acceptance and appreciation of each other cannot be abolished, but the limits they impose must be transcended. In Christ's body, all must welcome and value each others as "members one of another" (Ephesians 4:25). All whom God values as his children we must value as brothers; all who with us are limbs of Christ's body we should cherish as we do our own body (see 1 Corinthians 12:25ff.; Ephesians 5:28ff.). Jesus pinpoints practical concerns for the lowliest and neediest of his disciples, just because they are his disciples, as a vital virtue, a necessary element in genuine Christianity. (See Matthew 10:42; 25:34-45; cf. James 1:27.)

You might not think it from watching what goes on in our churches, but God wants life in his new society to be a perfect riot of affection, goodwill, openheartedness, and friendship. (So what on earth are we all playing at? You tell me!)

(2) *Service.* Service is love in action. Christ's body, says Paul, "upbuilds itself in [through, by means of] *agape* [love]" (Ephesians 4:16). *Agape* in Scripture is more than sweet talk or sweet smiles; its measure is the evil that you avoid inflicting, and the good you go out of your way to give. How then is the church upbuilt—that is, edified—in love? By "each part . . . working properly" in *koinonia* (fellowship). *Koinonia* means giving and taking according to the marvelous formula

of the Communist Manifesto—"from each according to his ability; to each according to his need." What by God's gift we have and are is for sharing—not hoarding!

This sharing is the *diakonia* (service, ministry) to which every Christian is called. Preachers and pastors are provided, says Paul, "that Christians may be properly equipped for their service." (Ephesians 4:12, Phillips). The gifts (i.e., powers to serve) which all Christians receive from the Holy Spirit must be used to the full for others' good.

Called to Minister

Edifying (the upbuilding of the body) is corporate: either we all advance towards Christlike maturity together, through mutual ministry (layfolk to layfolk and to clergy too, as well as vice versa), or we all stagnate separately. So a great deal depends on our hearing that call to Christian ministry which our baptism has issued to us all.

Note:

[1]*The Anglican Prayer Book*

Further Bible Study

Serving in Christ's body:
- Ephesians 4:7-16
- 1 Corinthians 12:14-13:13

Questions for Thought and Discussion

- What is the source and the form of the Christian's "extraordinary life"?
- The Bible says that there are no racial, social, or sexual distinctions in Christ. How then should we act toward one another?
- Why is it true that we either advance together or stagnate separately? Do you think this is right? Why?

13

Baptism Improved

Nobody doubts (how could one?) that the Christian's creed must shape his life. But we seem not to see that the same is true of his baptism. Yet if baptism really signifies God's grace giving salvation and our faith grasping it, the rite has to be a life-shaper; and Christians knew this yesterday, even if we miss it today. Thus, the Puritans taught folk to "make use of" and "improve" their baptism: that is (whatever their words might suggest to modern readers), to make it fuel for their faith, hope, love, joy, and obedience. This is a lesson we too should learn.

Seven Meanings

There are seven ways in which I, as a believer, should view my baptism.

First, it was a *gospel* service, in which "the power of God for salvation to every one who has faith" (Romans 1:16) was set forth in symbol, and God gave me a personal guarantee that through faith I might experience that power. As surely as I passed under the water then, so surely is the new life in Christ there for my asking now. So my baptism assures me that each day I may know more of supernatural deliverance from evil—guilt, doubt, fear, bitterness, hostility, misery, crippling habits, moral weakness, despairing loneliness (which is not the same as isolation, but is a reaction to it), and so on.

Second, my baptism was a *marriage* service, in which I was given away to Jesus my Lord to be his person, his covenant-partner, "for better, for worse"—but ultimately for the best (his best!), and forever. So my baptism reminds me whose I am and whom I must serve; who it is that stands pledged to love and cherish me, and share with me eternally all that he has, and what love and loyalty I owe in return.

Death-Day

Third, my baptism was a *burial* service, a funeral rite committing the man I was by nature, in Adam, to total destruction. "We were buried therefore with him [Christ] by baptism [that is, by the work of God revealed in baptism] . . . united with him in a death like his," for "our old self was crucified with him so that the sinful body [not just the physical organism, but also the disordered urges that stir it] might be destroyed [rendered powerless]" (Romans 6:4-6). So my baptism calls upon me not to live "according to the flesh" [that is, self-deifying inclination], but always "by the Spirit [to] put to death the deeds of the body" (Romans 8:12ff.).

Fourth, my baptism was an *Easter* festival, proclaiming both Jesus' resurrection and mine, as a believer, in and with his. "In baptism . . . you were also raised with him through faith in the working of God, who raised him from the dead" (Colossians 2:12). Through the indwelling Spirit I am truly risen already, though I must await Christ's return for my raising to be physically complete. Meantime, my baptism requires me to show forth day by day the Christ-life which now courses through me, while at the same time confirming to me that a new and better body will be mine.

Birthday

Fifth, my baptism was a *birthday* celebration: I might say, my official "new-birth-day," for new birth is what co-resurrection with Christ effects. As the Queen's official birthday is not her actual anniversary, so the day of the Christian's new birth, when he knowingly committed himself to a known Christ, will not ordinarily have been the day of his baptism (for infants that could hardly be, and for adults a profession of new birth must precede baptism). Yet, as all birthdays are times for delight at life's goodness, so my baptism should teach me constant joy at being spiritually alive in Christ.

Sixth, my baptism was an *admission* ceremony, bringing me into the family of God's adopted children so that I might share the family life of worship, witness, and work for our Father's glory. So my baptism should give me a sense of oneness, and a call to practical identification, with the people who are the real salt of the earth—those who belong to God's church, and specially that segment of it with which I worship each Sunday.

Seventh, my baptism was a *commissioning* service, entering me upon a life wholly given to serve Christ and his cause. In his epitaph, written by himself, John Berridge, the eighteenth-century evangelical leader, called himself Christ's errand-boy. That is what my baptism committed me to be.

So brooding, and digesting these conclusions, I shall "improve" my baptism—and the same goes for you, too!

Further Bible Study

Outward sign and inward reality:
- Romans 2:17-29

Questions for Thought and Discussion

- What did the Puritans mean by "improving" one's baptism?
- In what way is baptism a "gospel service"? How is the candidate personally involved in this?
- How can baptism be both a burial service and a birthday celebration? Is this a contradiction in terms? Why or why not?

14

Third Birthday

My baptism looks on to my third birthday. What is that? It is the day entered from eternity in God's private calendar, as my first two birthdays were, on which my heart is due to stop beating.

When or how it will happen I do not know—whether after or without warning, whether while I am nearer nineteen than 90, whether at home, in hospital, or out of doors, whether peacefully or in agony, whether through natural decay as described in Ecclesiastes 12, or through some killing disease, or human violence or miscalculation, or even through Christ's return to end this world. All I know is that some day, some way, my heart will stop, as sure as eggs are eggs, and that what the world will call my death-day will really be a birthday—the third in line.

Life to Come

What were my other two birthdays? Number one was when I left the womb, to see and feel and feed and shout as an inhabitant of this physical world; number two was when I came from spiritual darkness eighteen years later to see and feel and feed and shout about God's salvation, and Christ's love for me. By "birthday," you see, I mean not an anniversary, but a day that sees me start enjoying gifts of God such as I had never before imagined. That is what heartstop

day will bring; that is why my death-day will truly be a birthday.
Said D. L. Moody: "Someday they'll tell you Moody's dead. Don't
you believe it! That day I'll be before the throne; I'll be more alive
than I've ever been." Yes; and so shall I.

A friend wrote: "O God, I am so grateful that I have asked you
to be in control of my life, to be my authority, my Lord; I am so
relieved that the decision is not mine to choose the time to write
'death,' 'finish' to this earthly walk; for, in my humanity, in my
unknowing foolishness, I might choose never to choose! . . . For
death is truly a door to more instead of less, a plus instead of a
minus, an increase instead of a decrease, a filling instead of an emptying, a birthday instead of a wake!" Exactly.

We look on death as an exit, a way out from the light we love into
a hateful darkness. So it is for unbelievers, but for Christians death
is an entrance, a way leading from twilight here (spiritually, life here
is never more than that) into the sunshine of seeing our God. "They
stand before the throne of God and minister to him day and night
in his temple; and he who sits on the throne will dwell with them.
They shall never again feel hunger or thirst, the sun shall not beat
on them nor any scorching heat, because the Lamb who is at the
heart of the throne will be their shepherd and will guide them to
the springs of the water of life; and God will wipe all tears from
their eyes" (Revelation 7:15-17, NEB).

As Paul said, "to depart and be with Christ . . . is far better"
(Philippians 1:23). A Christian's death is promotion, not tragedy,
however early in life it comes; the mourners weep for themselves,
and for those left behind. When Bunyan's Christiana died, "her
Children wept, but Mr. Great-heart, and Mr. Valiant"—two men of
faith who knew what death was about—"played upon the well-
tuned Cymbal and Harp for Joy." "If we knew what God knows
about death," said George MacDonald, "we would clap our hands."

Sign of Hope

How can I be sure of all this? First, from my Bible; second, from
my baptism. Jews were landlubbers, and in Scripture water (waves,
depths, storms) is often an emblem of chaos and death. "Water
closed over my head; I said, 'I am lost'" (Lamentations 3:54). So in
baptism going under water signifies dying with Jesus physically, as

well as morally by repentance and self-denial, and emerging from the water is a sign of continuance with Jesus after death into physical resurrection, as well as being a token of spiritual renewal now.

Thus the rite of baptism is an acted promise from God that death will not end my existence or my joy, for a new gift of life will override the death sentence; and the fact that I was passive when God's minister baptized me teaches me that I may and must depend on God's active grace thus to bring me home. God's promise to me in my baptism extends to my deathbed and after, when the Lord Jesus takes me to himself (John 14:1-3; 17:24). When Browning wrote "the best is yet to be," he was right. My third birthday is still to come.

Further Bible Study

Welcome home!:
- John 14:1-4
- Luke 23:39-43
- 1 Peter 1:1-9
- 2 Peter 1:1-11

Questions for Thought and Discussion

- Do you agree that death is a birthday, not a wake? Explain your meaning.
- How does the prospect of death differ for Christians and non-Christians?
- What does our baptism tell us about our death?

Part Three

Learning To Pray:
The Lord's Prayer

The Lord's Prayer
"Pray then like this:
Our Father who art in heaven,
Hallowed by thy name.
Thy kingdom come,
Thy will be done,
On earth as it is in heaven.
Give us this day our daily bread;
And forgive us our debts,
As we also have forgiven our debtors;
And lead us not into temptation,
But deliver us from evil.
[For thine is the kingdom and the power
and the glory, for ever. Amen."]

(MATTHEW 6:9-13)

Material in brackets is found in some ancient manuscripts, though not all.

Preface

Three venerable formulae, as we are seeing, together add up to Christianity: the Creed, the Ten Commandments, and the Lord's Prayer, summarizing respectively the Christian way of believing, behaving, and communing with God.

The Lord's Prayer in particular is a marvel of compression, and full of meaning. It is a compendium of the gospel (Tertullian), a body of divinity (Thomas Watson), a rule of purpose as well as of petition, and thus a key to the whole business of living. What it means to be a Christian is nowhere clearer than here.

Like other Reformation catechisms, the Anglican Prayer Book Catechism centers on the three summaries. On the Lord's Prayer it says:

Question: What desirest thou of God in this prayer?
Answer: I desire my Lord God our heavenly Father, who is the giver of all goodness, to send his grace unto me, and to all people, that we may worship him, serve him, and obey him, as we ought to do. And I pray unto God, that he will send us all things that be needful both for our souls and bodies; and that he will be merciful unto us, and forgive us our sins; and that it will please him to save and defend us in all dangers ghostly (i.e., spiritual) and bodily; and that he will keep us from all sin and wickedness, and from our ghostly enemy, and from everlasting death. And this I trust he will do of his mercy and goodness, through our Lord Jesus Christ. And therefore I say, Amen. So be it.

What these words give us a glimpse of, the following studies will try to spell out.

1

When You Pray

Praying to God is a problem for many today. Some go through the motions with no idea why; some have exchanged prayer for quiet thought or transcendental meditation; most, perhaps, have given prayer up entirely. Why the problem? The answer is clear. People feel a problem about prayer because of the muddle they are in about God. If you are uncertain whether God exists, or whether he is personal, or good, or in control of things, or concerned about ordinary folk like you and me, you are bound to conclude that praying is pretty pointless, not to say trivial, and then you won't do it.

But if you believe, as Christians do, that Jesus is the image of God—in other words, that God is Jesus-like in character—then you will have no such doubts, and you will recognize that for us to speak to the Father and the Son in prayer is as natural as it was for Jesus to talk to his Father in heaven, or for the disciples to talk to their Master during the days of his earthly ministry.

Two-Way Conversation

Conversations with parents or wise friends whom we love and respect, and who are ready to help us by advice and action, feel neither pointless nor tedious, and we gladly give time to them—indeed, schedule time for them—because we value them, and gain from them. This is how we should think of times of communion with God in prayer. When the Methodist saint Billy Bray said, as he often did, "I must talk to Father about that," it was of praying that he spoke.

Does God, then, really tell us things when we pray? Yes. We shall probably not hear voices, nor feel sudden strong impressions of a message coming through (and we shall be wise to suspect such experiences should they come our way); but as we analyze and verbalize our problems before God's throne, and tell him what we want and why we want it, and think our way through passages and principles of God's written Word bearing on the matter in hand, we shall find many certainties crystallizing in our hearts as to God's view of us and our prayers, and his will for us and others. If you ask, "Why is this or that happening?" no light may come, for "the secret things belong to the Lord our God" (Deuteronomy 29:29); but if you ask, "How am I to serve and glorify God here and now, where I am?" there will always be an answer.

Made to Pray

It is not too much to say that God made us to pray; that prayer is (not the easiest, but) the most *natural* activity in which we ever engage; and that prayer is the measure of us all in God's sight. "What a man is alone on his knees before God," said the saintly Murray McCheyne, "that he is—and no more."

Perhaps Jesus' disciples felt this when they made their momentous request (have you ever echoed it?), "Lord, teach us to pray" (Luke 11:1). Jesus must have rejoiced to be asked this. In the manner of a good teacher, however, he controlled his feelings and gave a matter-of-fact answer. "When you pray, say . . ."—and for the second time in his public ministry he gave them the form of words which we call the Lord's Prayer (Luke 11:2-4; cf. Matthew 6:9-13).

"Say . . . " Did Jesus just intend that they should repeat the words, parrot fashion? No; but that they should enter into the sense. "Say," we might say, means "mean!" This prayer is a pattern for all Christian praying; Jesus is teaching that prayer will be acceptable when, and only when, the attitudes, thoughts, and desires expressed fit the pattern. That is to say: every prayer of ours should be a praying of the Lord's Prayer in some shape or form.

Learning to Pray

"Experience can't be taught!" The phrase comes from a brochure on youth employment, but it is as deep a truth about prayer as it is about wage-earning skills. Praying, like singing, is something you learn to do, not by reading books (not even this one!), but by actually doing it; and it is so natural and spontaneous an activity that you can become quite proficient in it without ever reading it up. Yet, as voice training helps you to sing better, so others' experience and advice can help us pray to better purpose. The Bible is full of models for prayer: 150 patterns of praise, petition, and devotion are contained in the Psalter, and many more examples of proper praying are recorded too, along with much teaching on the subject.

We should certainly not content ourselves with parroting off other people's prayers, nor would God be content if we did (for what parent could be happy if his child only ever spoke to him in quotations, thus limiting his conversation to the reciting of other people's sentiments?) But as another pianist's interpretation of a piece can help a budding musician to see how he can best play it (not, perhaps, in quite the same way), so we are helped to find our own way in prayer by seeing how others have prayed, and indeed by praying with them. And overarching everything we have the Lord's Prayer as our guide.

As analysis of light requires reference to the seven colors of the spectrum that make it up, so analysis of the Lord's Prayer requires reference to a spectrum of seven distinct activities: *approaching* God in adoration and trust; *acknowledging* his work and his worth, in praise and worship; *admitting* sin, and seeking pardon; *asking* that needs be met, for ourselves and others; *arguing* with God for blessing, as wrestling Jacob did in Genesis 32 (God loves to be argued with); *accepting* from God one's own situation as he has shaped it; and *adhering* to God in faithfulness through thick and thin. These seven activities together constitute biblical prayer, and the Lord's Prayer embodies them all.

So the Lord's Prayer should be put to service to direct and spur on our praying constantly. To pray in terms of it is the sure way to keep our prayers within God's will; to pray through it, expanding the clauses as you go along, is the sure way to prime the pump when prayer dries up and you find yourself stuck. We never get beyond this prayer; not only is it the Lord's first lesson in praying, it is all the other lessons too. Lord, teach us to pray.

Further Bible Study

The naturalness of prayer:
- Psalm 27; 139

Questions for Thought and Discussion

- How does one's view of God affect one's view of prayer?
- Why is prayer "the most natural activity in which we ever engage"?
- In what sense should every prayer be a mirror of the Lord's Prayer?

2

Pray Then Like This

P ray then like this." Thus Jesus introduced the Lord's Prayer in the Sermon on the Mount (Matthew 6:9-13). Clearly, then, the prayer is given us to be a pattern for our thoughts in prayer as well as a set verbal form. What does the pattern contain? Here is a bird's-eye view.

The address to God (invocation) with which the prayer opens is full of meaning. It must have startled the disciples, for in Judaism calling God "Father" was something one did not do. Jesus directs us, however, to do it—in other words, to seek access and welcome to God's presence on the ground that we are children in his family, and he looks on us with a father's love. Then with this we are to link the thought that our Father is "in heaven"—in other words, that he is God, sovereign and self-existent, the God who is both *there* and *in charge*. Fatherly love on the one hand, and transcendent greatness on the other, are two qualities in God which the rest of the prayer assumes at every point.

Then come three God-centered petitions, voicing together the attitude required by what Jesus called "the great and first commandment—you shall love the Lord your God with all your heart . . ." (Matthew 22:38, 37).

The first petition is that God's *name* should be hallowed. "Name" in the Bible means "person," and the hallowing of God's name means the acknowledging of God as holy through reverence for all his revelation and responsive worship and obedience.

The second petition is that God's *kingdom* should come. God's "kingdom" means the public display of his ruling power in salvation, and the prayer for his kingdom to come is a plea that his lordship might be seen and submitted to, and his saving grace experienced, all the world over, till Christ returns and all things are made new.

The third petition asks that God's *will* may be done—that is, that all his commands and purposes may be perfectly fulfilled.

God First, Then Man

Three man-centered petitions follow. By putting them after requests for the exalting of God, the prayer reminds us that we are to ask for the meeting of our particular personal needs *as a means to our Father's glory*, and not in any spirit of trying to bend God's will to our own. We are told to ask for provision of bread, pardon of sins, and protection from temptation and the tempter ("evil" means "the evil one"). All our needs are in principle covered here—all need for material things; all need for spiritual renewing and restoring; all need for guidance and help.

The "praise ending" ascribes to God the *kingdom* (that is, it hails him as God on the throne), the *power* (that is, it adores him as the God able to do all that we ask), and the *glory* (that is, it declares "we praise thee, O God" here and now). Though early, the manuscripts make it clear that it is not from Christ's own lips—but there is no denying that it fits!

God Leads The Conversation

When we talk to parents and friends about our anxieties and problems, looking to them for help, they often have to take over leadership in the conversation in order to give it a meaningful shape which our own higgledy-piggledy minds have denied it. We all know what it is to have been pouring out our troubles in full flood and to be pulled up by "Wait a minute; let's get this straight. Now tell me again about so-and-so . . . Now tell me how you felt about it . . . Then what's the problem?" Thus they sort us out.

We need to see that the Lord's Prayer is offering us model

answers to the series of questions God puts to us to shape our conversation with him. Thus: "Who do you take me for, and what am I to you?" (*Our Father in heaven.*) "That being so, what is it that you really want most?" (*The hallowing of your name; the coming of your kingdom; to see your will known and done.*) "So what are you asking for right now, as a means to that end?" (*Provision, pardon, protection.*) Then the "praise ending" answers the question, "How can you be so bold and confident in asking for these things?" (*Because we know you can do it and when you do it, it will bring you glory!*) Spiritually, this set of questions sorts us out in a most salutary way.

Sometimes when we pray we feel there is nobody there to listen, and are tempted to think that our feelings tell us the truth. What finally dispels this temptation, under God, is a fresh realization (Spirit-given, for sure) that God is actually questioning us in the way described, requiring us to tell him honestly how we think of him and what we want from him and why.

That this is so is part of the teaching of the Lord's Prayer, which from this standpoint is like a child's picture containing a hidden object. At first you look and don't see the object; then it hits you, and every time you look at the picture after that it seems to jump out at you. The hidden object in this case is the God who asks the questions to which the Lord's Prayer, clause by clause, is the proper set of answers. And it is only when you see this that you can use the pattern prayer in the way that its Author and Teacher intended.

Further Bible Study

A model prayer:
- John 17

Questions for Thought and Discussion

- On what basis should we seek access to God's presence? Do you think you have such access yourself? What are your reasons for saying yes or no?
- What does the Lord's Prayer have to do with loving God with all our heart?
- Illustrate ways in which the Lord's Prayer might be needed to reshape prayers that we might make.

3

Our Father

The Lord's Prayer is in family terms: Jesus teaches us to
invoke God as our Father, just as he himself did—witness
his Gethsemane prayer, for instance, or his High Priestly
prayer in John 17, where "Father" comes six times. A question,
however, arises. Jesus was God's Son by nature, the second person
of the eternal Godhead. We, by contrast, are God's creatures. By
what right, then, may we call God *Father*? When Jesus taught this
manner of address, was he implying that creaturehood, as such,
involves sonship—or what?

Adopted

Clarity here is vital. Jesus' point, as we saw in an earlier study, is not
that all men are God's children by nature, but that his committed
disciples have been adopted into God's family by grace. "To all who
received him, who believed in his name, he gave power to become
children of God" (John 1:12). Paul states this as the purpose of the
incarnation: "God sent forth his Son . . . so that we might receive
adoption as sons" (Galatians 4:4, 5). Prayer to God as Father is for
Christians only.

This resolves a puzzle. Elsewhere, Jesus stressed that his disciples should pray in his name and through him; that is, looking to
him as our way of access to the Father. See John 14:6, 13; 15:16;

16:23-26. Why is there none of this in the model prayer? In fact, the point is present here; it is implicit in "Father." Only those who look to Jesus as Mediator and sin-bearer, and go to God through him, have any right to call on God as his sons.

Sons and Heirs

If we are to pray and live as we should, we must grasp the implications of God's gracious fatherhood.

First, as God's adopted children we are *loved* no less than is the one whom God called his "beloved Son" (Matthew 3:17; 17:5). In some families containing natural and adopted children the former are favored above the latter, but no such defect mars the fatherhood of God.

This is the best news anyone has ever heard. It means that, as Paul triumphantly declares, nothing " ... in all creation, will be able to separate us from the love of God in Christ Jesus our Lord" (Romans 8:39). It means that God will never forget us, or cease to care for us, and that he remains our forbearing Father even when we act the prodigal (as, alas, we all sometimes do).

It means too that, as the Prayer Book says, he is "always more ready to hear than we to pray," and is "wont to give more than either we desire or deserve." "If you then, who are evil," said our Lord, "know how to give good gifts to your children, how much more will your Father who is in heaven give good things to those who ask him!" (Matthew 7:11; the parallel saying in Luke 11:13 has "Holy Spirit" for "good things," and the sustained ministry of the Holy Spirit was surely one of the good things Jesus had in mind.) To know this truth of God's fatherly love to us gives boundless confidence not merely for praying, but for all our living.

Second, we are God's *heirs*. Adoption in the ancient world was for securing an heir, and Christians are joint heirs with Christ of God's glory (Romans 8:17). "We are God's children now ... when he appears we shall be like him" (1 John 3:2). Already "all (things) are yours" in the sense that they further your good here and your glory hereafter, for "you are Christ's" (1 Corinthians 3:21-23; Romans 8:28-30). To grasp this is to know oneself rich and privileged beyond any monarch or millionaire.

Third, we have *God's Spirit* in us. With our changed relationship to God (adoption) goes a change of direction and desire, of outlook and attitude, which Scripture calls regeneration or new birth. Those who "believed in" Jesus' "name" were "born . . . of God" (John 1:12ff.), or more precisely "born of the Spirit" (3:6; see verses 3-8). "Because you are sons," says Paul, "God has sent the Spirit of his Son into our hearts, crying [that is, prompting us to cry, spontaneously, as the expression of a new spiritual instinct], 'Abba! Father!'" (Galatians 4:6). And when, to our distress (and this comes to us all), we find ourselves so muddle-headed, dead-hearted, and tongue-tied in prayer that "we do not know how to pray as we ought," then our very desire to pray as we should and our grief that we are not doing so shows that the Spirit is himself making effective intercession for us in our hearts (Romans 8:26ff.); which is as reassuring as it is mysterious, and as thrilling as it is amazing.

Fourth, we must *honor* our Father by serving his interests. The center of our concern must be "thy name . . . kingdom . . . will," and we must be like good children in human families, ready to obey instructions.

Fifth, we must love our *brothers*, by constant care and prayer for them. The Lord's Prayer schools us in intercession for the family's needs: "Our Father . . . give us . . . forgive us . . . lead us . . . deliver us . . . " "Us" means more than just me! For God's child, prayer is no "flight of the alone to the Alone," but concern for the family is built into it.

So we should be expressing faith in Christ, confidence in God, joy in the Holy Spirit, a purpose of obedience, and concern for our fellow Christians when we go to God and call him "Father." Only so shall we answer Jesus' intention in teaching us this form of address.

Praise and Thanks

As invocation of God as Father opens this pattern prayer, so renewed realization of the family relationship—his parenthood, and our sonship by grace—should always come first in our practice of prayer. All right-minded praying starts with a long look Godward and a deliberate lifting up of one's heart to give thanks and adore, and it is just this that "Father" calls us to. Thanks for grace, and praise for God's paternity, and joy in our sonship and heirship should bulk large in Christian prayer, and if we never got beyond it we should still be praying to good purpose. First things first!

So I ask: Do we always pray to God as Father? And do we always praise when we pray?

Further Bible Study

God's fatherhood:
- Romans 8:12-25
- Matthew 6:1-16

Questions for Thought and Discussion

- What gives us the right to call God our Father? Why may only Christians do this?
- What is the importance of realizing our sonship to God when we pray?
- Why would one say, "The Lord's Prayer schools us in intercession for the family's needs"?

4

Which Art in Heaven

The vitality of prayer lies largely in the vision of God that prompts it. Drab thoughts of God make prayer dull. (Could this be your problem?) A book was once published with the title *Great Prayers of the Bible*: the mark of great prayers, in the Bible or elsewhere, is that they express a great awareness of a great God.

The invocation of God in the Lord's Prayer draws us into just such an awareness. "Our Father" speaks of the quality and depth of God's love to Christ's people—all the sustained care and concern that a perfect father could show. "Which art in heaven" sets before us the fact that our divine Father is great—eternal, infinite, almighty: thus it makes us realize that God's love is unchanging, unlimited, unconquerable in its purpose, and more than able to deal with all the needs we bring when we pray. Prayer shaped and supported by thoughts like this will not be dull

Heaven

Since God is spirit, "heaven" here cannot signify a place remote from us which he inhabits. The Greek gods were thought of as spending most of their time far away from earth in the celestial equivalent of the Bahamas, but the God of the Bible is not like this. Granted, the "heaven" where saints and angels dwell has to be thought of as a sort of locality, because saints and angels, as God's creatures, exist in space and time; but when the Creator is said to be "in heaven" the thought is that he exists on a different *plane* from us, rather than in a different *place*. That God in heaven is always near to his children on earth is something which the Bible takes for granted throughout.

Worship

Knowledge of God's greatness should both humble us (cut us down to size!) and move us to worship. The Lord's Prayer was meant to teach us, not just to ask for things, but also to worship God for all that he is, and thus to *hallow his name* in our own hearts. Angels and saints in glory worship God as Father (Ephesians 3:14ff.), and so on earth must we.

Knowing that our Father God is in heaven, or (putting it the other way round) knowing that God in heaven is our Father, is meant to increase our wonder, joy, and sense of privilege at being his children and being given the "hot line" or prayer for communication with him. "Hot line" it truly is, for though he is Lord of the worlds, he always has time for us; his eye is on everything every moment, yet we always have his full attention whenever we call on him. Marvelous! But have we really taken it in? It merits much thought, and there are two roads along which our minds can travel in order to grasp it properly.

Either: think first of God's greatness, as the infinite and eternal Creator who "dwells in unapproachable light" (1 Timothy 6:16), apparently remote. Think of Solomon's question, "Will God dwell indeed with man on the earth? Behold, heaven and the highest heaven cannot contain thee . . . " (2 Chronicles 6:18). But then think of what is in effect God's reply to Solomon: "Thus says the high and lofty One who inhabits eternity, whose name is Holy: 'I dwell in the high and holy place, and also with him who is of a contrite and humble spirit . . . '" (Isaiah 57:15). And then remind yourself that this promise finds its deepest fulfillment when God becomes the Father of insignificant sinful mortals like us, sinners who are *contrite* in repentance and *humble* in acknowledging their illdesert and fleeing by faith to Jesus for refuge. For this awesome, holy, transcendent God stoops down in love to lift us up from the gutter, so to speak, brings us into his family, gives himself to us in unstinting fellowship, and thus enriches us forever.

Or: think of God's fatherhood, and then remind yourself that he is "in heaven" (a "heavenly" Father, as we say); which means that he is free from all the limitations, inadequacies, and flaws that are found in earthly parents, and that his fatherhood, like all his other relationships, is from every standpoint absolutely ideal, perfect and glorious. Dwell on the fact that there is no better father, no parent more deeply committed to his children's welfare, or more wise and generous in promoting it, than God the Creator.

Let your thoughts move to and fro like an accelerating pendulum, taking ever wider swings. "He's my Father—and he's God in heaven; he's God in heaven—and he's my Father! It's beyond belief—but it's true!" Grasp this, or rather, let it grasp you; then tell God what you feel about it; and that will be the worship which our Lord wanted to evoke when he gave us this thought-pattern for the invocation of the One who is both his Father and ours.

Further Bible Study

In touch with God transcendent:
- Isaiah 40

Questions for Thought and Discussion

- What is the importance of the fact that the God to whom we pray is in heaven?
- What is meant by saying that God "exists on a different plane from us, rather than in a different place"? What does this tell us about God?
- What response should a knowledge of God's greatness evoke in us?

5

Hallowed Be
Thy Name

ere we left to ourselves, any praying we did would both
start and end with ourselves, for our natural self-cen-
teredness knows no bounds. Indeed, much pagan praying of this kind goes on among supposedly Christian people. But
Jesus' pattern prayer, which is both crutch, road, and walking lesson for the spiritually lame like ourselves, tells us to start with God:
for lesson one is to grasp that God matters infinitely more than we
do. So "thy" is the keyword of the opening three petitions, and the
first request of all is "hallowed (holy, sanctified) be *thy name*"—
which is the biggest and most basic request of the whole prayer.
Understand it and make it your own, and you have unlocked the
secret of both prayer and life.

Glory Be To God

What does "hallowed be thy name" ask for? God's "name" in the
Bible regularly means the *person* he has revealed himself to be.
"Hallowed" means known, acknowledged, and honored as holy.
"Holy" is the Bible word for all that makes God different from us,
in particular his awesome power and purity. This petition, then,

asks that the praise and honor of the God of the Bible, and of him only, should be the issue of everything.

The idea that "glory be to God alone" is a motto distinguishing John Calvin and his admirers is no discredit to them, but it is a damning sideswipe at all other versions of Christianity. In truth, however, every school of Christian thought insists, more or less clearheadedly, that the praise of God, as distinct from the promoting of ourselves, is the proper purpose of man's life. "Not unto us, O Lord, but unto thy name give glory" (Psalm 115:1).

A Sense of Direction

Who can pray this request and mean it? Only he who looks at the whole of life from this point of view. Such a man will not fall into the trap of superspirituality, so concentrating on God's redemption as to disregard his creation; people like that, however devoted and well-meaning, are unearthly in more senses than one, and injure their own humanity. Instead, he will see everything as stemming ultimately from the Creator's hand, and therefore as fundamentally good and fascinating, whatever man may have made of it (beauty, sex, nature, children, arts, crafts, food, games, no less than theology and church things). Then in thankfulness and joy he will so live as to help others see life's values, and praise God for them, as he does. Supremely in this drab age, hallowing God's name starts here, with an attitude of gratitude for the goodness of the creation.

But it does not stop here. Hallowing God's name requires praise for the goodness and greatness of his redemptive work too, with its dazzling blend of wisdom, love, justice, power, and faithfulness. By wisdom God found a way to justify the unjust justly; in love he gave his Son to bear death's agony for us; in justice he made the Son, as our substitute, suffer the sentence that our disobedience deserved; with power he unites us to Christ risen, renews our hearts, frees us from sin's bondage, and moves us to repent and believe; and in faithfulness he keeps us from falling, as he promised to do (see John 10:28ff.; 1 Corinthians 1:7ff.; 1 Peter 1:3-9), till he brings us triumphantly to our final glory. We do not save ourselves! Neither the Father's saving grace, nor the Son's saving work, nor our own saving faith originate with us; all is God's gift. Salvation, first to last, is of the Lord, and the hallowing of God's name requires us to acknowledge this, and to praise and adore him for the whole of it.

Nor is this all. God's name is only fully hallowed when he is worshiped for ordering all things for his people's ultimate good (cf. Romans 8:28), and also for the truth and trustworthiness of his written Word, which every believer should prize as "a lamp to my feet and a light to my path" (Psalm 119:105). "Thou hast exalted thy word above all thy name," says the Psalmist (138:2, margin), and so responsively must we. God's name—meaning, God himself—is dishonored if his children live in fear, as if their Father had lost control of his world, or in uncertainty, as if they dare not follow their Elder Brother's example and receive the teaching and promises of the Bible as instruction from the Father himself. There is, unhappily, widespread failure today to hallow God's name in these ways.

The hallowing throughout is by *gratitude*; what dishonors God is non-appreciation and lack of gratitude, which Paul pinpoints as the root cause of men's falling away from God (Romans 1:20ff.). It is by being, not merely knowledgeable, but grateful, and by expressing gratitude in thankful obedience, that we honor and glorify our Maker. "Hallowed be thy name" expresses the desire that we ourselves and all rational beings with us should give God glory in this way.

Scripture calls the spirit which hallows God's name the "fear" of the Lord, hereby signifying awe and esteem for God's majesty on the one hand and humble trust (yes, trust, not mistrust or scaredness!) on the other. A classic text here is Psalm 111. "Praise the Lord . . . Great are the works of the Lord . . . full of honor and majesty . . . faithful and just; all his precepts are trustworthy . . . he has commanded his covenant for ever. Holy and terrible is his name!" And then, "The fear of the Lord [the response of praise for God's works and words, which the psalm has been voicing] is the beginning of wisdom" (discernment of the way to live).

The old term of respect, "God-fearing" (rarely used today, perhaps, because there are few to whom it would apply), normally carried the implication of good sense and mature humanity as well as that of godliness, and thus reflected our fathers' awareness that the two go together; true reverence for God's name leads to true wisdom, realistic and shrewd, and when Christians appear goofy and shallow one has to ask whether they have yet learned what the hallowing of God's name means.

Man's Chief End

"Man's chief end," says the Shorter Catechism, magnificently, "is to glorify God, and to enjoy him for ever." End, note, not ends; for the two activities are one. God's chief end, purposed in all that he does, is his glory (and what higher end could he have?), and he has so made us that we find our own deepest fulfillment and highest joy in hallowing his name by praise, submission, and service. God is no sadist, and the principle of our creation is that, believe it or not (and or course many don't, just as Satan doesn't), our duty, interest and delight completely coincide.

Christians get so hung up with the pagan idea (very dishonoring to God, incidentally) that God's will is always unpleasant, so that one is rather a martyr to be doing it, that they hardly at first notice how their experience verifies the truth that in Christian living duty and delight go together. But they do!—and it will be even clearer in the life to come. To give oneself to hallowing God's name as one's life-task means that living, though never a joy ride, will become increasingly a joy *road*. Can you believe that? Well, the proof of the pudding is in the eating! Try it, and you will see.

Further Bible Study

God's name glorified:
* Psalm 148

Questions for Thought and Discussion

* How does the Lord's Prayer differ from prayers we would form if left to ourselves?
* In your own words, what does it mean to hallow God's name?
* How does the belief that all comes ultimately from God affect one's outlook on life?

6

Thy Kingdom Come

That "the Lord is king" in the sense of being sovereign over his world is assumed throughout the Bible. But God's king-ship and his king*dom* are different things. The former is a fact of creation, commonly called providence; the latter is a reality of redemption, properly called grace.

This distinction is biblical in substance, but the vocabulary of Scripture does not show it. *Kingdom* is used in both Testaments for both God's universal sovereign sway and his redemptive relation-ship to individuals through Jesus Christ. In the Lord's Prayer, "thy kingdom come" uses the word in the latter sense, "thine is the king-dom" in the former.

God in sovereignty overrules the lives and doings of all men, including those who deliberately defy and disobey him. In a mon-strous outburst of sibling rivalry surpassed only by Cain's fratricide, Joseph's brothers sold him into slavery and told his father Joseph was dead. Yet God was overruling, so that later Joseph could say, "You meant evil against me; but God meant it for good" (Genesis 50:20). "By the hands of lawless men" the Jews of Jerusalem "cru-cified and killed" Jesus; yet God was overruling, so that Jesus was "delivered up according to the definite plan and foreknowledge of God," and by his death the world was redeemed (Acts 2:23).

But this overruling is a different thing from God's reign of grace in the heart and life of one who bows in penitent trust before his authority, desiring only to be delivered from evil and led in paths of righteousness. And that is precisely how it is when we make Jesus king.

Jesus and the Kingdom

So God's kingdom is not a place, but rather a relationship. It exists wherever people enthrone Jesus as lord of their lives. When Jesus began preaching that "the kingdom of God is at hand" (literally, "has drawn near") he meant that the long-promised enjoyment of God's salvation for which Israel had been waiting was now there for them to enter into (Mark 1:15). How were they to enter it? The Gospels answer that question very fully. Why, by becoming Jesus' disciples; by giving him their hearts' loyalty, and letting him reshape their lives; by receiving forgiveness from him; by identifying with his concerns; by loving him without reserve, and giving his claims precedence over all others—in short, by manifesting what Paul called "faith working through love" (Galatians 5:6), faith which acknowledges and embraces Jesus Christ as, in Peter's phrase, "Lord and Savior" (2 Peter 1:11; 2:20; 3:2, 18).

To this faith Jesus pointed Nicodemus (John 3:13-15), having told him that no one sees or enters the kingdom without a radical inner transformation by the Spirit which he pictured as being "born again" (verses 3-8). The passage instructs us that none of us can enter the kingdom without the Spirit's help, and we must not be too proud to ask for it, nor refuse to be changed in whatever ways God sees necessary.

The kingdom arrived with Jesus; indeed, one might say that as Son of God incarnate, Jesus is the kingdom of God in person. His rule over Christians is regal in the full-blooded biblical sense, personal, direct, and absolute. His claims are the claims of God, overriding those of man. Yet his rule is not tyranny, for King Jesus is his people's servant, their shepherd and champion, ordering all things for their protection and enrichment. "My yoke is easy, and my burden is light" (Matthew 11:30).

Also, he is their brother in the royal family, who himself lived on earth as "a man under authority" (Matthew 8:9); he will not ask more of us than was asked of him; indeed, not so much. His rule has the nature, not of dictatorship, but of pastoral care. "I am the good shepherd; I know my own" (John 10:14).

The first and fundamental service rendered by "great David's greater Son" to his disciples is to save them from sin and death, according to God's promise. So the kingdom of God is the realm of grace, where the damage done to us by sin is repaired; and the gospel of grace proves to be what the kingdom is all about.

Present and Future

In one sense, the kingdom is here now, and Christians are in it. But in another sense—that of perfecting the display of God's grace in this world—the kingdom remains future, and awaits Christ's return. The prayer "thy kingdom come" looks on to that day. But this does not exhaust its meaning. Any request for a new display of God's sovereignty in grace—renewing the church, converting sinners, restraining evil, providing good in this world—is a further spelling out of "thy kingdom come." If one asks where in the Lord's Prayer does general intercession appear, the answer is here. (And if one asks, Why burden oneself with a load of intercession? the answer is, Because we are taught to pray, "Thy kingdom come.")

The Personal Challenge

To pray "thy kingdom come" is searching and demanding, for one must be ready to add, "and start with me; make me your fully obedient subject. Show me my place among 'workers for the kingdom of God' (Colossians 4:11), and use me, so far as may be, to extend the kingdom and so be your means of answering my prayer." Made sincerely, this is a prayer that the Savior who calls to self-denial and cross-bearing and consent that one's life be lost, one way or another, in serving the gospel, may have his way with us completely. Do we really seek this? Have we faced it? Let every man examine himself, and so—only so—let him say the Lord's Prayer.

Further Bible Study

The kingdom of God (=heaven):
● Matthew 13:1-52

Questions for Thought and Discussion

- Do you agree that "God's kingdom is not a place, but a relationship"? Why or why not?
- Why can we rightly say that Jesus was (and is) a king but not a tyrant?
- Think out the present-day implications of the prayer "thy kingdom come," so far as you are able to see them.

7

Thy Will Be Done

Every word of the Lord's Prayer reflects the Lord's vision of what our lives should be—unified, all-embracing response to the love of our heavenly Father, so that we seek his glory, trust his care, and obey his word, every moment of every day. If, therefore, we are to pray the Lord's Prayer with understanding and sincerity, we must make this vision our own. So when I say "hallowed be thy name; thy kingdom come," I should be adding in my mind the words "in and through me," and so giving myself to God afresh to be, so far as I can be, the means of answering my own prayer. And when I say "thy will be done," I should mean this as a prayer that I, along with the rest of God's people, may learn to be obedient.

Here more clearly than anywhere the purpose of prayer becomes plain: not to make God do my will (which is practicing magic), but to bring my will into line with his (which is what it means to practice true religion).

Not My Will

So understood, "thy will be done" takes some praying! I cannot sincerely ask for the doing of God's will without denying myself, for when we get down to the business of everyday living, we regularly find that it is our will rather than his that we want to do, or to see

179

happening. Nor can I pray this prayer without dedicating myself to keep loyal to God in face of all the opposition which in this fallen world, where Satan is "prince" (John 14:30), I regularly meet. Luther expounded the words like this: "Let thy will be done, O Father, not the will of the devil, or of any of those who would over-throw thy holy Word or hinder the coming of thy kingdom; and grant that all we may have to endure for its sake may be borne with patience and overcome, so that our poor flesh may not yield or give way from weakness or laziness." For God's will to be done in our lives *on earth* in the way that it is done among the angels will involve us in quite a struggle.

See what this petition meant when Jesus voiced it in Gethsemane (Matthew 26:42). The incarnate Lord was in the grip of mind-blowing horror, evoked not just by the expectation of physical pain and outward disgrace (strong men can bear these things in a good cause without too much ado), but by the prospect of being *made sin* and forsaken by his Father on the cross. "Never man feared death like this man," said Luther, truly; and this was why. His whole being shrank from it; yet his prayer remained "not as I will, but as thou wilt" (v. 39). What it cost him to pray thus we shall never know. What it may cost us to accept God's will we cannot say either—which is, perhaps, as well.

Accepting God's Will

The Greek for "be done," in both the Lord's Prayer and the Gethsemane story, is literally "happen," and God's will here is two things, his purpose for events and his command to his people. In relation to the former, "thy will be done" expresses the spirit of meekness, which accepts without complaining whatever God sends, or fails to send. In relation to the latter, we are asking God to teach us all that we should do and make us both willing and able for the task. Can you pray this from the heart? It is not so easy as it looks.

Finding God's Will

But how shall we know what God wants of us? By paying attention to his Word and to our own consciences, by noting what circum-stances allow, and by taking advice in order to check our own sense of the situation and the adequacy of our insight into what is right. Problems about God's will regularly come clear as they are bounced off other Christian minds. One's own inner state is important too. "If any man's will is to do (God's) will," not only will he know that Jesus and his teaching are from God (John 7:17), but he will be told if he is out of the way. "Your ears shall hear a word behind you, saying, 'This is the way, walk in it,' when you turn to the right or when you turn to the left" (Isaiah 30:21). If you are open to God, God will get through to you with the guidance you need. That is a promise!

While you are unclear as to God's will, wait if you can; if you have to act, make what you think is the best decision, and God will soon let you know if you are not on the right track.

A Covenant With God

Here, in closing, are some extracts from the superb Covenant Service of the Methodist Church, which say exactly what you and I should now be saying. Following a reminder that in the New Covenant God promises us "all that he declared in Jesus Christ," while we for our part "stand pledged to live no more unto ourselves," the leader says:

"O Lord God, Holy Father, who has called us through Christ to be partakers of this gracious Covenant, we take upon ourselves with joy the yoke of obedience, and engage ourselves, for love of Thee, to see and do thy perfect will."

Then all the worshipers join in words which John Wesley took from the Puritan, Richard Alleine, for this purpose in 1755:

"I am no longer my own, but Thine. Put me to what Thou wilt, rank me with whom Thou wilt; put me to doing, put me to suffering; let me be employed for Thee or laid aside for Thee, exalted for Thee or brought low for Thee; let me be full, let me be empty; let me have all things, let me have nothing; I freely and heartily yield all things to Thy pleasure and disposal.

"And now, O glorious and blessed God, Father, Son and Holy Spirit, Thou art mine, and I am Thine. So be it. And the Covenant which I have made on earth, let it be ratified in heaven. Amen."

Further Bible Study

The will of God:

- Acts 20:16–21:14

Questions for Thought and Discussion

- What is prayer's true purpose? Is this why you pray?
- What does prayer have to do with denying ourselves?
- What are some of the problems involved in finding God's will for our lives, and how should we deal with them?

8

On Earth As It Is in Heaven

Three doctrinal statements bind the Lord's Prayer together. The first two come in the invocation. God is the Father of Christian people, and he is in heaven. The third rounds off the first trio of petitions: in heaven God's will is done. The first proclaims God's goodness in redeeming us through the cross and taking us into his family. The second and third declare his greatness and power to achieve his purpose. Together, these three truths point up the Christian hope. As our Father, God stands pledged to love us and do us good for all eternity.

Heaven

As Lord of creation, ruling in heaven, i.e., in freedom from the limitations of space-time creaturehood here on earth, God can be relied on to fulfill his intention perfectly. You and I are capable of failing in anything we undertake, however simple, but it is God's glory to succeed in all that he has set himself to do, however hard. So

> *The work which his mercy began*
> *The arm of his strength will complete;*
> *His promise is yea and amen,*
> *And never was forfeited yet.*

Things future, nor things that are now,
Not all things below or above,
Can make him his purpose forego,
Nor serve my soul from his love.

But when Jesus says that in heaven God's will is done, he is not thinking so much of our Father's transcendence as of a community of created beings, intelligent like ourselves, living nearer to God (in the sense that they enjoy more of him than we can in this world), and serving him with an ecstatic wholeheartedness that in this life we never attain. This is "heaven" in the most usual sense of the word, the "heaven" to which Christians "go" when they die, the state of life for which our time here is all preparation and training.

Heaven in this sense is infinitely more important than the present life, not only because it is endless while this life is temporary, but also because no relationships are perfectly enjoyed here in the way that they will be hereafter. From the fact that the Holy Trinity is the ultimate reality, no less than from the insights of present-day psychologists, we learn that relationships are what life—real life, as distinct from mere consciousness—is really all about, and relationships, with Father, Son, and saints, are certainly what heaven is all about. It is no accident that the New Testament presents heaven as a city (Revelation 21), a banquet (Matthew 8:11; Luke 22:29ff.; Revelation 19:9), and a worshipping congregation (Hebrews 12:22-24; cf. Revelation 7:9-17); these pictures are telling us that heaven will be an experience of *togetherness*, closer and more joyous than any we have known so far, whether with our God or with our fellow-believers.

In *The Great Divorce*, C. S. Lewis imagines hell as a country where people are always scattering to get as far from each other as they can! (And Sartre in *No Exit* pictured hell as other people from whom one can never get away, however hellishly they behave.) But in heaven the saints will be close to each other, as well as to the Father and the Son—and glad to be; and the closeness will add to the joy.

With robust emphasis, Scripture is "other-worldly," insisting that the life of heaven is better and more glorious than life on earth at every point. But when we ask just how, Scripture says to us in effect, "Wait and see (cf. Romans 8:24); and realize that it is so far beyond your present experience that you really can't conceive it." Heaven, being an order of reality not bounded by space and time as we know them, is not located in, nor can be defined by, this present world in which our physical nature anchors us. All we are sure of is that, as we said, for heaven's inhabitants (the "ministering spirits" who are angels, with "the spirits of just men made perfect") it is a state of perfect communion with God, and with others in God, and complete contentment in his presence. That is the further truth the Bible pictures of the golden city and the great feast are meant to convey.

But for perfect communion not only must God give without limit or restraint; his servants, angelic and human, must also respond without reserve—which means that in and through them God's will is fully done. The doing of God's will is thus part of the definition of heaven, and it is part of heaven's glory that God gives those who are there full ability to do it.

Praise

Why did Jesus follow "thy will be done on earth" with "as it is in heaven"? Surely for two reasons.

First, he wants at this point to arouse *hope*. The chaos of earth mocks the petition; by reminding us, however, that God has already established his will perfectly in heaven, Jesus stirs us to hope that on earth we may yet see great things. "Is anything too hard for the Lord?" (Genesis 18:14).

Nor is this all. Jesus' second aim is to awaken *praise*. While petition exhausts, praise invigorates, and for Jesus to interpose between two spells of arduous petition a moment to pause and praise—"in heaven, Father, your will is done! hallelujah!"—is the spiritual equivalent of refreshment at half-time, whereby strength for the battle of intercession is renewed. Here Jesus teaches the precious lesson that *praising energizes and renews praying*. Hear him!

Further Bible Study

Earth and Heaven:
- Hebrews 12

Questions for Thought and Discussion

- What is the significance of God's not being limited by space and time?
- What are the necessary elements of perfect communion with God?
- What is meant by the phrase "while petition exhausts, praise invigorates"?

9

Our Daily Bread

Having focused on God's name, kingdom, and will, the Lord's Prayer turns attention to our meals. Is this a letdown? Not at all: it is a genuine progression.

For, firstly, those who truly pray the first three petitions thereby commit themselves to live wholly for God, and the natural and logical next request is for food to give them energy for this. Dr. Johnson's reply to the criticism that he cared much for his stomach was that those who ignore the needs of their stomach are soon in no condition to care about anything else. Christian realism? Yes, just that.

Secondly, we do in fact depend every moment on our Father-Creator to keep us and the rest of the universe in being (for without his will nothing could still exist), and to sustain nature's rhythmical functioning so that each year sees seedtime, harvest, and food in the shops (cf. Genesis 8:22); and it is right for us to acknowledge this dependence regularly in prayer, particularly in an age like ours which, having assumed nature to be self-sustaining, now has problems about the reality of God.

Some regard petitions for personal material needs as low-grade prayer, as if God were not interested in the physical side of life and we should not be either. But such hyper-spirituality is really an unspiritual ego-trip; see how in Colossians 2:23 Paul warns that man-made asceticism does not stop indulgence of the flesh (i.e., the sinful self). Petitions looking to God as the sole and omnicompetent source of supply of all human needs, down to the most mundane, are expressing truth, and as the denying of our own self-sufficiency humbles us, so the acknowledging of our dependence honors God. Neither our minds nor our hearts are right till we see that it is as necessary and important to pray for daily bread as for (say) the forgiveness of sins.

Thirdly, God really is concerned that his servants should have the food they need, as Jesus' feedings of the 4,000 and 5,000 show. God cares about physical needs no less than spiritual; to him, the basic category is that of *human* needs, comprising both.

The Body

This petition shows us how to regard our bodies. The Christian way is not to deify them, making health and beauty ends in themselves, as modern pagans do; nor is it to despise them, making scruffiness a virtue, as some ancient pagans (and Christians too, unfortunately) once did. It is rather to accept one's body as part of God's good creation, to act as its steward and manager, and gratefully to enjoy it as one does so. Thus we honor its Maker. Such enjoyment is in no way unspiritual for Christ's disciples; for them, it is like their salvation, the Lord's free gift.

The Bible opposes all long-faced asceticism by saying that if you enjoy health, good appetite, physical agility, and marriage in the sense that you have been given them, you should enjoy them in the further sense of delighting in them. Such delight is (not the whole, but) part of our duty and our service of God, for without it we are being simply ungrateful for good gifts. As Screwtape truly said (with disgust), "He's a hedonist at heart": he values pleasure, and it is his pleasure to give pleasure. Well did some Rabbis teach that at the judgment God will hold against us every pleasure that he offered us and we neglected. Do we yet know how to enjoy ourselves—yes, physically too—to the glory of God?

Material Needs

Note that we are to pray for *our* daily bread. There is intercession for other Christians here as well as petition for oneself. And "bread," man's staple diet in both the ancient and the modern worlds, stands here for all life's necessities and the means of supplying them. Thus, "bread" covers all food; so the prayer is for farmers and against famine. Again, the prayer covers clothing, shelter, and physical health; so the prayer becomes an intercession for social and medical services. Or again, the prayer covers money and power to earn, and so becomes a cry against poverty, unemployment, and national policies which produce or prolong both. Luther wished that rulers put loaves rather than lions in their coats of arms, to remind themselves that their people's welfare must come first, and he urged that it is under this clause of the Lord's Prayer that prayer for those in authority most properly comes.

Daily

J. B. Phillips correctly rendered this clause "give us this (each) day the bread we need." We are told to ask for bread, as the Israelites were told to gather manna, on a day-to-day basis: the Christian way is to live in constant dependence on God, a day at a time. Also, we are to ask for the bread we *need*; i.e., for the supply of necessities, not luxuries we can do without. This petition does not sanctify greed! Moreover, we must as we pray be prepared to have God show us, by his providential response of not giving what we sought, that we did not really need it after all.

Now comes the real test of faith. You, the Christian, have (I assume) prayed for today's bread. Will you now believe that what comes to you, much or little, is God's answer, according to the promise of Matthew 6:33? And will you on that basis be content with it, and grateful for it? Over to you.

Further Bible Study

God provides:
- Psalm 104
- Matthew 6:19-34

Questions for Thought and Discussion

- Do you agree that God is as concerned about physical needs as he is about spiritual ones? Why or why not?
- As good stewards, what attitudes should we have toward our own bodies?
- Why, and in what sense, is Christianity meant to be a day-at-a-time life?

10

Forgive Us

The Christian lives through forgiveness. This is what justification by faith is all about. We could have no life or hope with God at all, had God's Son not borne the penalty of our sins so that we might go free. But Christians fall short still, and forgiveness is needed each day; so Jesus in part two of his model prayer included a request for it between the pleas for material provision and spiritual protection. This reflects nothing in his own praying, for he knew he was sinless (cf. John 8:46); it is here for us.

Debts

How should Christians see their sins? Scripture presents sins as lawbreaking, deviation, shortcoming, rebellion, pollution (dirt), and missing one's target, and it is always all these things in relation to God; but the special angle from which the Lord's Prayer views it is that of unpaid debts. "Forgive us our debts, as we also have forgiven our debtors" is the RSV rendering of Matthew 6:12 (see also Luke 11:4 and the parable of the two debtors, Matthew 18:23ff.). Those denominations that say "trespasses" instead of "debts," echoing Luke 11:4, unfortunately miss this point. Jesus' thought is that we owe God total tireless loyalty—zealous love for God and men, all day and every day, on the pattern of Jesus' own—and our sin is basically failure to pay. The Anglican Prayer Book rightly confesses sins of omission ("we have left undone those things which we ought to have done") before sins of commission: the omission perspective is basic. When Christians examine themselves, it is for omissions that they should first look, and they will always find that their saddest sins take the form of good left undone. When the dying Archbishop Usher prayed, "Lord, forgive most of all my sins of omission," he showed a true sense of spiritual reality.

Sinning Sons

A problem arises here. If Christ's death atoned for all sins, past, present, and future (as it did), and if God's verdict justifying the believer ("I accept you as righteous for Jesus' sake") is eternally valid (as it is), why need the Christian mention his daily sins to God at all? The answer lies in distinguishing between God as Judge and as Father, and between being a justified sinner and an adopted son. The Lord's Prayer is the family prayer, in which God's adopted children address their Father, and though their daily failures do not overthrow their justification, things will not be right between them and their Father till they have said "sorry" and asked him to overlook the ways they have let him down. Unless Christians come to God each time as returning prodigals, their prayer will be as unreal as was that of the Pharisee in Jesus' parable.

Intolerable

Here emerges a lesson: Christians must be willing to examine themselves and let others examine them for the detecting of day-to-day shortcomings. The Puritans valued preachers who would "rip up" the conscience; more such preaching is needed today. The discipline of self-examination, though distasteful to our pride, is necessary because our holy Father in heaven will not turn a blind eye to his children's failings, as human parents so often (and so unwisely) do. So what he knows about our sins we need to know too, so that we may repent and ask pardon for whatever has given offense.

From one standpoint, Christians' shortcomings offended most of all, just because they have most reason (the love of God in Christ) and most resources (the indwelling Holy Spirit) for avoiding sinful ways. Those who think that because in Christ their sins are covered they need not bother to keep God's law are desperately confused (see Romans 6). As it upsets a man more to learn that his wife is sleeping around than that the girl next door is doing it, so God is most deeply outraged when his own people are unfaithful (see Hosea's prophecy, especially chapters 1-3). "This is the will of God, your sanctification" (1 Thessalonians 4:3)—and nothing less will do.

The Communion Service in the 1662 Prayer Book teaches Christians to call the "burden" (guilt) of their sins "intolerable." The justification for this strong language is knowledge of the intolerable grief brought to God by the sins of his own family. How sensitive are we to this? And how concerned that, as sons of God, our lives should be so far as possible sin-free? The true Christian will not only seek to find and face his sins through self-examination, but he will labor "by the Spirit" to "put to death the deeds of the body" (i.e., the habits of the old sinful self) all his days (Romans 8:13).

Only the Forgiving are Forgiven

Those who hope for God's forgiveness, said Jesus, must be able to tell him that they too have forgiven their debtors. This is not a matter of earning forgiveness by works, but of qualifying for it by repentance. Repentance—change of mind—makes mercy and forbearance central to one's new life-style. Those who live by God's forgiveness must imitate it; one whose only hope is that God will not hold his faults against him forfeits his right to hold others' faults against them. Do as you would be done by is the rule here, and the unforgiving Christian brands himself a hypocrite. It is true that forgiveness is by faith in Christ alone, apart from works, but repentance is faith's fruit, and there is no more reality in a profession of faith than there is reality of repentance accompanying it. Jesus himself stresses that only those who grant forgiveness will receive it in Matthew 6:14ff.; 18:35.

So again the question is: can I say the Lord's Prayer? Can you? We shall all do well to make the following lines a plea of our own:

"Forgive our sins as we forgive,"
—you taught us, Lord, to pray;
but you alone can grant us grace
to live the words we say.

> How can your pardon reach and bless
> the unforgiving heart
> that broods on wrongs, and will not let
> old bitterness depart?
>
> In blazing light your Cross reveals
> the truth we dimly knew,
> how small the debts men owe to us,
> how great our debt to you.
>
> Lord, cleanse the depths within our souls,
> and bid resentment cease;
> then, reconciled to God and man,
> our lives will spread your peace.

Further Bible Study

Asking forgiveness:
- Psalm 51

Qualifying for forgiveness:
- Matthew 18:23-35

Questions for Thought and Discussion

- How does the Lord's Prayer define sin? How is this seen in our daily living?
- Why does a person need to confess daily sins after he becomes a Christian?
- Why can unforgiving Christians rightly be called hypocrites?

11

Not into Temptation

After prayer for provender and pardon comes a cry for protection, our third basic need. The sentence has two halves; "lead us not into temptation, but deliver us from evil" (either sin, or trouble, or both, or "the evil one" who manipulates trouble to induce sin). Both halves, however, express a single thought: "life is a spiritual minefield; amid such dangers we dare not trust ourselves; Father, keep us safe." Here the Lord's Prayer links up with the view of life that runs through the Psalms. The realism, self-distrust, and humble dependence on God that breathes through this petition is something we all need to learn.

Testing

The thought that God may lead Christians into temptation, as the first clause assumes, has puzzled and shocked many people. Things grow clearer, however, once we see what temptation means here. "Test" or "trial"—that is, a situation which reveals how far you are able to go right and avoid going wrong—is the idea behind the word. The driving test, which (believe it or not) is designed to enable you to show that you can do everything right, is a "temptation" in this sense. Now, any educational or training program must of necessity include periodic tests for gauging progress, and the experience of taking and passing such tests can be very encouraging to the trainee.

In God's program for the spiritual education and growth of Christians, the same applies. God does and must test us regularly, to prove what is in us and show how far we have got. His purpose in this is wholly constructive, to strengthen us and help us forward. Thus he "tested" Abraham (so RSV; AV has "tempt," RV "prove") by telling him to sacrifice Isaac, and after the test promised him great blessing "because you have obeyed my voice" (Genesis 22:1, 18).

No Picnic

Why, then, if temptation is beneficial, should we ask to be spared it? For three reasons. First, whenever God tests us for our good, Satan, "the tempter," tries to exploit the situation for our ruin. "Your adversary the devil prowls around like a roaring lion, seeking someone to devour" (1 Peter 5:8). Jesus knew from his wilderness experience how mean and cunning Satan is, and wished no one to underestimate him or to court a meeting with him. (Our modern occultists would do well to take this to heart.)

Second, the pressures in times of trial can be so appalling that no sane Christian can do other than shrink from them, just as they shrink from the thought of having cancer. For both reasons Jesus was as right to start his prayer in Gethsemane with "Father, remove this cup" as he was to end it with "yet not my will but yours be done" (cf. Matthew 26:39). Temptation is no picnic!

Third, knowledge of our own proven weakness, thickheadedness, and all-round vulnerability in spiritual matters, and of the skill with which Satan exploits our strong and weak points alike, mixing frontal assaults on our Christian integrity with tactics of infiltration and ambush, so that while avoiding one hazard we constantly fall victim to another, compels us to cry, in humility and self-distrust, "Lord, if it be possible, *please*, no temptation! I don't want to risk damaging myself and dishonoring you by falling!" Temptation may be our lot, but only a fool will make it his preference; others will heed Paul's warning to the spiritually reckless, "let any one who thinks that he stands take heed lest he fall" (1 Corinthians 10:12).

Watch and Pray

When Jesus found his disciples asleep in Gethsemane, he said, "Watch and pray that you may not enter into [that is, start yielding to] temptation; the spirit indeed is willing [to do God's will], but the flesh [human nature] is weak" (Matthew 26:41). What prompted his comment was the struggle he had just had with himself, in which his own flesh had violently recoiled from the prospect of Calvary, plus now the sleep of those who, though tired, had been asked to watch with him—stay awake, that is, and support him by their presence and prayers. We must appreciate that the test of sincerity and realism in saying "lead us not into temptation" is readiness to "watch and pray," lest we fall victim to it unawares.

"Watch" suggests a soldier on guard, alert for the first signs of enemy attack. We *watch* against temptation by noting what situation, company, and influences expose us to it, and avoiding them wherever we can. As Luther said, you can't stop the birds flying over your head, but you can stop them nesting in your hair. Find out what for you is fire, and don't play with it!

"Pray" points to the kind of prayer Jesus had just made—prayer for strength to do what one knows is right in face of inward reluctance plus any number of siren-songs seeking to charm one off course and spiritually onto the rocks.

Nobody ever expressed the right state of mind in this matter better than Charles Wesley, in the hymn that starts, "Jesus, my strength, my hope, On thee I cast my care."

> *I want a godly fear,*
> *A quick-discerning eye*
> *That looks to thee when sin is near*
> *And sees the tempter fly;*
> *A spirit still prepared*
> *And armed with jealous care,*
> *For ever standing on its guard*
> *And watching unto prayer.*

The conclusion of the matter is this. For good and necessary reasons connected with our Christian growth (cf. James 1:2-12), we shall not be spared all temptation (cf. 1 Corinthians 10:13); but if we ask to be spared and watch and pray against Satan's attempts to exploit situations for our downfall, we shall be tempted less than we might have been (cf. Revelation 3:10), and will find ourselves able to cope with temptation when it comes (1 Corinthians 10:13). So do not be unrealistic in not budgeting for temptation, nor foolhardy enough to court it; but when it comes, do not doubt God's power to deliver from the evil it brings, and to "keep you from falling" (Jude 24) as you pick your way through it. When you are not conscious of temptation, pray "lead us not into temptation"; and when you are conscious of it, pray "deliver us from evil"; and you will live.

Further Bible Study

Eve's temptation:
- Genesis 3:1-7

Abraham's temptation:
- Genesis 22:1-19

Jesus' temptation:
- Luke 4:1-15

Questions for Thought and Discussion

- What is "temptation," as the word is used here?
- What is God's purpose in testing us? How do you respond to such testing?
- Why should we ask to be spared from temptation?

12

Deliver Us

The vision of life in God's family which we learn from the Lord's Prayer has three dimensions. It is a life of devotion, of dependence, and of danger. "Deliver us from evil" is a plea for protection in face of danger that threatens—dangers that appear throughout the New Testament as constantly threatening the Christian believer.

Danger

In our comfortable routines of life we do not think of ourselves as being in danger. But we should; for we are. Once more, the Anglican Prayer Book provides much insight. Thus, the Litany expands "deliver us from evil" into five distinct petitions, and among the evils specified, side by side with circumstantial troubles, are these:

"From sin, from the crafts and assaults of the devil . . . from all blindness of heart; from pride, vain-glory and hypocrisy; from envy, hatred, and malice, and all uncharitableness . . . from fornication, and all other deadly sin; and from all the deceits of the world, and flesh, and the devil . . . from sudden [unexpected, and unprepared-for] death . . . from hardness of heart, and contempt of thy Word and Commandment, *Good Lord, deliver us.*"

Now we see what our deepest dangers are, and whence they arise. The deliverance we need is not only or mainly from adverse circumstances, but from the spiritual evil within us which makes both adverse and favorable circumstances its springboard for attack. Sin in our hearts, spawning all kinds of inclinations to do something other than God's will and to love something or someone more than God himself, is the source of our danger. Always and everywhere, the danger of being led astray by indwelling sin remains.

Deceit

Look again at the extract quoted from the Litany. All the evils listed flow spontaneously from the fallen human heart. Satan may be their ringmaster, deciding in what order they shall come on for their performance, but he does not have to inject them into our system; they are already there. And sin works for the most part by deceit. "Blindness . . . deceits . . . hardness of heart" are the keywords on sin's methods, as "pride . . . hypocrisy . . . uncharitableness" are the keywords on sin's manifestations. But pride and uncharitableness will masquerade as zeal for God, his truth, and his church—and other moral and spiritual evils will regularly creep in unnoticed while our attention is on something else. This is the way of what a Puritan called "the mystery of self-deceiving," and what Hebrews calls "the deceitfulness of sin" (Hebrews 3:13).

Facing danger, sensible men keep cool but go carefully, keeping alert, watching each step and ready to cry "help" at the first sign of trouble. So too the sensible Christian will watch and pray, lest he enter into temptation (see Matthew 26:41), and the cry for deliverance from evil will often be on his lips. And then he will be kept safe.

Deliverance

The television program, "This Is Your Life," reviewed each guest's personal history from the outside, in terms of work done and friends made. But if you were asked, "What is your life?" you would speak from the inside and go deeper. As a human being, you are a creature of purpose, and you would willy-nilly describe your life in terms of goals you have had, and of challenges, conflicts, frustrations, and progress in pursuit of them.

The secular, man-centered way of doing this is by estimating achievement and non-achievement, success and failure in tasks tackled. Memoirs and biographies of public figures review their careers in this way. Bible writers, Bible characters, and biblical Christians, however, do differently.

To start with, they look at their lives God-centeredly. They see God as the One whose action has been the decisive factor shaping their lives, and as the only one who is able to assess what they have achieved. And they see his action in terms of two main concepts. The first is *mercy*: their lives appear to them as, in the words of the hymn, "mercy from first to last." The second concept is *deliverance*: they see themselves as having been delivered over and over again from trouble and opposition that threatened to keep them from, or obstruct them in, God's service and their fellowship with him. God "delivered us from so deadly a peril [the Asian affliction], and he will deliver us; on him we have set our hope that he will deliver us again" (2 Corinthians 1:10): so spoke Paul, and his sentiment is typical of the whole Bible view of life, according to which hope for mercy and deliverance from evil, sin within and storms without, is an essential element in faith at all times. A little time with a concordance exploring the Bible uses of "deliver" and "deliverance" will convince you of this.

Can you yet see your own life in terms of being threatened and endangered by evil of all sorts, and so of needing God's deliverance every moment? If not, believe me, you cannot yet see what you are looking at! You are like a person wandering blindfolded and with ears plugged in the middle of a city street, with traffic coming both ways. Learn from the Lord's Prayer what is really going on in your life, and as you are increasingly enabled to discern the dangers, lean harder on the Great Deliverer. "Because he cleaves to me in love, I will deliver him"—that is God's promise to each saint (Psalm 91:14). Claim it; it is for you.

Further Bible Study

A song of deliverance:
- 2 Samuel 22 (= Psalm 18)

Questions for Thought and Discussion

- What does the fact that we must regularly pray for spiritual protection tell us about our lives?
- What is meant by the phrase "the spiritual evil within us which makes both adverse and favorable circumstances its springboard for attack"?
- What is meant by the Puritan phrase, "the mystery of self-deceiving"?

13

From Evil

The first thing to say about evil is that it is a reality, and we should not pretend that there is no such thing. Christian Scientists, like Hindu mystics, want to think it away as an illusion; others would see it as good in the making, or good misunderstood; but in the Bible evil is as real as good, and the distinction between them is ultimate.

The second thing to say about evil is that it is an irrational and meaningless reality, making no sense, and only definable as good perverted.

The third thing to say about evil is that God is handling it. At the cost of Calvary he has taken responsibility for bringing good out of it; already he has triumphed over it, and eventually he will eliminate it. The Christian contemplating evil is not a pessimist, for he knows that one day this mad and meaningless reality which destroys good shall be destroyed itself. Christ ensured this by conquering cosmic evil on the cross (see Colossians 2:15); he will finally snuff it out at his return.

On that day, the Christian expects to see that out of all his embroilments with the evil in and around him has come greater good for him, and greater glory for God, than could have been otherwise. That will finally vindicate the goodness and wisdom of God in giving evil so long a run in his world.

Two Sorts of Evil

Evil means badness which has the effect of ruining, or wasting, or ruling out, goodness—that is, the achieving of a life that is upright, worthwhile, and joyful. Evil, as defined, takes two forms. First, there is badness external to us, the badness of circumstances, "trouble, sorrow, need, sickness, or any other adversity." Circumstances become evil when they inflict on us more pain and frustration than we can turn into good by the way that we take them. In fact, circumstances are not often that bad. Beethoven was able to turn the frustration of deafness and the pain of loneliness into the music of heroism; countless invalids have been able to achieve dignity and serenity despite chronic physical agony; and the psalmist can say, "It is good for me that I was afflicted, that I might learn thy statutes" (Psalm 119:71). Yet when, as sometimes happens, pain is such that a man can only scream till he faints from exhaustion, this is surely evil.

Second, there is badness within us, the badness of corruption. This is the badness of bad men and fallen angels, the badness which is from one standpoint a lack of good and from another good gone wrong: as in the devil, in Adam, and in you and me. How and why good corrupts is more than Scripture explains or than we can grasp, but the fact is there. And whereas in relation to the first sort of evil we are passive, suffering it, in relation to the second sort we are active, doing it. "The evil I do not want is what I do," says Paul (Romans 7:19); to which every honest man's response must be, "Yes, and so do I."

God to the Rescue

Christians cannot disregard evil around and within them, nor are they at liberty to try, for their calling is to face evil and overcome it with good (Romans 12:21). But this assumes that evil does not overcome them; and here the Lord's Prayer comes in once more.

Jesus tells us to ask God to deliver us "from the evil." Whether this Greek phrase means "evil" in general (so RSV text) or "the evil one" (so RSV margin) does not matter, though the second is perhaps likelier. The first rendering would mean "deliver us from all the evil in the world, in ourselves, in other men, in Satan and his hosts"; the second rendering would mean "deliver us from Satan, who seeks our ruin, and from all that he exploits to that end—all the ungodliness of the world, all the sinfulness of our flesh, all spiritual evil of every sort"; both renderings come to the same thing.

And the great point is that Jesus' act of giving us this prayer is an implicit promise that if we seek deliverance from evil, we shall find it. The moment we cry "deliver," God's rescue operation will start; help will be on the way to cope with whatever form of evil threatens us.

Further Bible Study

Delivered from evil:
- 2 Corinthians 1:3-11; 12:1-10

Questions for Thought and Discussion

- What is God doing now about evil? What will he do ultimately?
- What determines whether evil circumstances make or break us?
- Whom does God deliver from evil, and why?

14

The Kingdom and the Power

As music can express the whole range of human feelings, so our Lord's pattern prayer covers the whole range of concerns with which life confronts the Christian disciple. Praise for our redemption (*Father*), adoration of God's transcendent greatness (*in heaven*), zeal for his glory (*hallowed be thy name*), longing for his triumph (*thy kingdom come*), and self-dedication to him (*thy will be done*) are all expressed in the first half; in terms of the common analysis of the elements of prayer as Adoration, Consecration, Thanksgiving and Supplication (making the mnemonic A-C-T-S), all save the last are now covered. Then the supplications of the second half have expressed our reliance on God for material needs (*give us . . . our daily bread*), our repentance over failures in faithfulness and our renouncing of mercilessness as a way of life (*forgive us . . . as we forgive*), and our sense of weakness in face of the forces of our spiritual foes (*lead us not into temptation, but deliver us*). Now, finally, following the traditional form of the prayer, we are led back to praise.

The doxology with which, following the older versions, we round off the Lord's Prayer is not in the best manuscripts.

Nevertheless, it is in the best tradition! Doxologies (that is, acts of praise to God for his glory) pop up all through the Bible, and we saw before how in personal devotion praise and prayer grow out of, lead into, and stir up each other. Need felt and need met are their respective mainsprings, and praise for what God is, and does, is the strong support of hope in what he can, and will, do. So the more you praise, the more vigor you will have for prayer; and the more you pray, the more matter you will have for praise.

Prayer and Praise

Prayer and praise are like a bird's two wings: with both working, you soar; with one out of action you are earthbound. But birds should not be earthbound, nor Christians praiseless. The clauses "who art in heaven" at the start and "as it is in heaven" in the middle are pauses for praise in the Lord's Prayer's flow, and if this closing doxology is not from Jesus' lips it certainly reflects his mind.

Praise is linked to prayer here by the conjunction "for": "for thine is the kingdom and the power and the glory . . . " The connection of thought is that we ask our heavenly Father for provision, pardon, and protection with great confidence, since we know that for him to give this to his children on the one hand is within his *capacity*, and on the other is in line with the character he shows when he deals with men—that is, his *glory*. This, therefore, is an actual instance of praise for God's power and glory coming in to undergird prayer for the fruits of both.

Kingdom and Power

Kingdom and power, as ascribed to God in this doxology, are two words expressing a single composite thought. (Grammarians call this idiom *hendiadys*: it is common in ancient literature.) The thought is of omnipotent control. Kingdom is used as in Psalm 103:19, "His kingdom rules over all": it denotes God's all-embracing mastery of the order of creation which is presupposed by the petition that God's kingdom in the other sense, the order of redemption touching everything, may "come." Satan, the prime example of how sin breeds cunning but saps intelligence and rots the mind, does not accept that the Lord is king in this basic sense, and would dismiss this doxology—indeed, all doxologies—as false; but Christians know better, and praise God accordingly.

Power is the actual mastery which God's rule shows: not, then, naked arbitrary power, like that of a tornado, or a rogue elephant, or a dotty dictator, but unconquerable beneficence, triumphantly fulfilling purposes of mercy and loving-kindness "to us and to all men." It is the power by which God is good to all, and rescued Israel from Egypt, and raised Jesus Christ from the dead (Ephesians 1:19ff., etc.).

Psalms proclaiming God as the invincible gracious King (Psalms such as 47, 93, 97, 145, for a start) form the best exposition of "the kingdom and the power" in this doxology. Read them, ponder them, get them under your skin and into your heart—and join the Christian glee club! "It is good to sing praises to our God; for he is gracious . . . " (Psalm 147:1).

Further Bible Study

God on the throne:
- Daniel 4
- Psalm 145

Questions for Thought and Discussion

- How do praise and prayer lead into and feed each other?
- What is "omnipotent control," and how is God exercising it in the world today?
- What is God's power like?

15

And the Glory

In the New Testament, the word "glory" carries two interlocked layers of meaning, each of which entails the other. Layer one is the manifested praiseworthiness of the Creator; layer two is the praise which this draws from his creatures. Which layer is "on top" depends on whether the reference is to the glory which God *has* and *shows* and *gives* or to that which he is given. For we in gratitude bless the God who in grace has blessed us, and this is to glorify the One who is even now glorifying us by remaking us in Christ's image (see 2 Corinthians 3:18; Ephesians 1:3; and compare Romans 1:21 with 8:17, 30). But that for which men give God glory is always something glorious, while the glories that God shows man are always intended to call forth praise.

Glory Seen

In the Old Testament, God displayed his glory in typical, visual form as an awe-inspiring expanse of bright light (the *shekinah*, as later Judaism called it). This was the sign of his beneficent presence in both the tabernacle and the temple (Exodus 40:34; 1 Kings 8:10ff.). The essential and abiding revelation of God's glory, however, was given by his great acts of merited judgment and unmerited love, and in his "name"—which was no mere label, as our names are, but a disclosure of God's nature and character. Jehovah (Yahweh, as modern scholars render it) means "I am (and will be) what I am (and will be)" (see Exodus 3:13-15), and the full statement of God's "name" declares precisely what he is and will be. This statement was made to Moses; when Moses asked God, "show me thy glory," God responded not only by a visual manifestation, but also by declaring "my name 'the LORD' (Yahweh) . . . a God merciful and gracious, slow to anger, and abounding in steadfast love and faithfulness, keeping steadfast love for thousands, forgiving iniquity and transgression and sin, but who will by no means clear the guilty . . . " (Exodus 33:18-34:7). This moral character is the essential glory of God.

So, when the Word was made flesh in lowliness, having emptied himself of the glory he shared with the Father before creation, the breathtaking brilliance of the *shekinah* was hidden, save for the one isolated moment of transfiguration; yet Jesus' disciples could testify, "we beheld his glory," the glory of personal deity "full of grace and truth" (John 1:14; cf. 17:5; Philippians 2:7). Great as is the physical glory of *shekinah* light, the moral glory of God's redeeming love is greater. Those today whom God enlightens to understand the gospel never see the *shekinah*, but they behold the glory of God in the face of Jesus Christ (2 Corinthians 4:6).

Glory Given

When in the traditional Lord's Prayer doxology we ascribe the glory, along with the royal rule, to God forever, we are, first, telling God (and thus reminding ourselves) that he, our Maker and Redeemer, is, and always will be, glorious in all he does, especially in his acts of grace ("we give thanks to thee *for thy great glory*"); and, second, we are committing ourselves, now and always, to worship and adore him for it all ("*glory be* to God on high"). The doxology thus makes the Lord's Prayer end in praise, just as the Christian life itself will do: for while petition will cease with this life, the happy task of giving God glory will last for all eternity.

Glory to Whom?

Now let us test our spiritual quality.

The principle of human sin (which is the devil's image in man) is this: glory is not God's, but mine. Accordingly, we parade what we think of as our glory, so that admiring watchers will give us glory.

This is one facet of our pride: we call it vanity. Vain persons put on a show with their features, physical shape, clothes, skills, position, influence, homes, brains, acquaintanceships, or whatever they are most proud of, expect applause, and feel resentful and hurt if people do not play up to them and act impressed.

But Christians know that vanity is a lie, for it assumes that it is we who should be praised and admired for what we are; and that is not so. Christianity teaches us, not indeed to pretend that we lack qualities which we know very well that we have, but to acknowledge that all we have is God's gift to us, so that he should be praised and admired for it rather than we.

The test is to ask yourself how pleased, or how displeased, you become if God is praised while you are not, and equally if you are praised while God is not. The mature Christian is content not to have glory given to him, but it troubles him if men are not glorifying God. It pained the dying Puritan, Richard Baxter, the outstanding devotional writer of his day, when visitors praised him for his books. "I was but a pen in God's hand," he whispered, "and what praise is due to a pen?" That shows the mentality of the mature; they want to cry every moment, "Give glory to God!—for it is his due, and his alone!"

What does this test tell us about ourselves?

Further Bible Study

The way of doxology:
- Romans 11:33-36
- Ephesians 3:20ff.
- 1 Timothy 6:13-16
- Hebrews 13:20ff.
- Jude 24ff.
- Revelation 1:4-7

Questions for Thought and Discussion

- What are the two meanings of the word "glory," and what is the relationship between the two?
- What does God's character have to do with his glory?
- Is our ability to see God's glory limited by the absence of the *shekinah*? Why or why not?

16

Amen

When we say "Amen" after the Lord's Prayer, or any other prayer, what does it mean?

Yes, That's the Truth!

"Amen" is a Hebrew word used in Old Testament and synagogue worship, whence it passed into Christian speech. In Scripture it not only ends prayer, showing an earnest wish to be heard, but also voices acceptance of such things as King David's orders (1 Kings 1:36) and God's threats (Numbers 5:22; Deuteronomy 27:17-26). Its root meaning is "true, firm, solid, certain," and what it expresses is an emphatic yes to what has been said: "definitely yes" as a man from the English Midlands might say, or "that's the truth" as in colloquial American. "So may it be," the usual paraphrase of "amen," is too weak: "amen" expresses not just a wish, but a committed confidence—"so *shall* it be."

"Amen" may either follow an utterance or precede it ("verily" in Jesus' formula, recurring more than fifty times, "verily I say . . ." is "amen" in the original). Either way, however, it underlines the utterance as an important one with which the speaker fully identifies. In 2 Corinthians 1:20, Paul speaks of Christians saying "amen" to God's promises, so glorifying him as true and trustworthy in what he says, "the God whose name is Amen" and whose "words are true" (Isaiah 65:16, NEB; 2 Samuel 7:28). Also, in Corinthians 14:16 he envisages Christians saying "amen" to prayers of thanks uttered in public worship. The effect of saying "amen," assuming it is said with heart no less than voice, is to associate oneself with both promises and prayers in a way that makes them one's own.

Your Prayer?

The traditional doxology teaches us to round off the Lord's Prayer with "amen." This is right. "Amen" (best said loudly and with emphasis) is our final profession of having meant what we have said, and identified completely with the attitudes, hopes, and goals that the prayer expresses. So the fittest way to end these brief studies in the prayer which takes a lifetime (and more) to master is with a checklist of the main items involved; and therefore I ask:

Do you identify with the trust in Jesus Christ as your own Savior, and the faith in God as your own God through him, and the recognition of every Christian as your own brother in God's family, which is expressed by "Our Father"?

Is the hallowing of God's name in and through you, whatever that may cost, your own controlling purpose in life? Do you want to see God triumph in his kingdom, and to see everything that does not match his perfection come to an end?

Will you labor and suffer for the kingdom, if need be, so as to become its agent, the means of bringing it into lives and situations where the gates have been locked against God?

Do you happily take God's will of command for your rule, and God's will of events for your destiny, knowing (by faith) that both are supremely good?

Is there any matter in which you are flying in the face of God's will of command, excusing yourself on the grounds of there being other commands which you faithfully keep? If so, what will you now do about it?

Do you see and know that unless God acts to provide for today's needs, and to pardon today's sins, and to protect you in today's temptations, you are lost?

Do you make it an issue of conscience never to bear a grudge or cherish bitterness against anyone, but to show forgiving mercy always, because of the forgiving mercy that God always shows you?

Is there any person whom hitherto you have refused to forgive for what he or she did to you? Will you ask the Lord this moment to help you change your attitude, and get right with that person?

Do you make it your habit to watch and pray against temptation? Will you make it your habit from now on?

Is the Lord's Prayer really in your heart? Are you being honest when you say "amen" to it? "O God, make clean our hearts within us; and take not thy Holy Spirit from us." Lord, teach me how to pray, by teaching me how to live; for Jesus' sake; *amen.*

Further Bible Study

The dangers of insincerity:
- Ecclesiastes 5:1-6
- Acts 5:1-11

Questions for Thought and Discussion

- What does "amen" mean?
- Why is God called "the God whose name is Amen"?
- What is involved in saying "Amen" to the Lord's Prayer?

Part Four

Design for Life:
The Ten Commandments

The Ten Commandments

And God spoke all these words, saying,

"I am the Lord your God, who brought you out of the land of Egypt, out of the house of bondage.

"You shall have no other gods before me.

"You shall not make for yourself a graven image, or any likeness of anything that is in heaven above, or that is in the earth beneath, or that is in the water under the earth; you shall not bow down to them or serve them; for I the Lord your God am a jealous God, visiting the iniquity of the fathers upon the children to the third and the fourth generation of those who hate me, but show steadfast love to thousands of those who love me and keep my commandments.

"You shall not take the name of the Lord your God in vain; for the Lord will not hold him guiltless who takes his name in vain.

"Remember the sabbath day, to keep it holy. Six days you shall labor, and do all your work; but the seventh day is a sabbath to the Lord your God; in it you shall not do any work, you, or your son, or your daughter, your manservant, or your maidservant, or your cattle, or the sojourner who is within your gates; for in six days the Lord made heaven and earth, the sea, and all that is in them, and rested the seventh day; therefore, the Lord blessed the sabbath day and hallowed it.

"Honor your father and your mother, that your days may be long in the land which the Lord your God gives you.

"You shall not kill.

"You shall not commit adultery.

"You shall not steal.

"You shall not bear false witness against your neighbor.

"You shall not covet your neighbor's house; you shall not covet your neighbor's wife, or his manservant, or his maidservant, or his ox, or his ass, or anything that is your neighbor's."

(EXODUS 20:1-17)

Preface

C ars are complex contraptions, and with their thousands of component parts much can go wrong. The maker's handbook, however, tells you how to get from your car a satisfying performance, with minimum wear and tear, and if you mishandle it so that it goes wrong, you cannot say that you were not warned. With the wisdom contained in the repair manual which the manufacturers also issue, the car can be mended, but as long as you pooh-pooh the maker's instructions, trouble is all you can expect.

Our cars are parables of their owners. We too are wonderfully made, complex physically and even more so psychologically and spiritually. For us, too, there is a maker's handbook—namely, God's summary of the way to live that we find in the Ten Commandments. Whether as persons we grow and blossom or shrink and wither, whether in character we become more like God or more like the devil, depends directly on whether we seek to live by what is in the Commandments or not. The rest of the Bible could be called God's repair manual, since it spells out the gospel of grace that restores sin-damaged human nature, but it is the Commandments that crystallize the basic behavior-pattern which brings satisfaction and contentment, and it is precisely for this way of living that God's grace rescues and refits us.

Suppose someone says: "I try to take the Ten Commandments seriously, and live by them, and they swamp me! Every day I fail somewhere. What am I to do?" The answer is: now that you know your own weakness and sinfulness, turn to God, and to his Son Jesus Christ, for pardon and power. Christ will bring you into a new kind of life, in which your heart's deepest desire will be to go

God's way, and obedience will be burdensome no longer. That folk who take the law as their rule might find Christ the Savior as their Ruler is something to pray and work for.

God's love gave us the law just as his love gave us the gospel, and as there is no spiritual life for us save through the gospel, which points us to Jesus Christ the Savior, so there is no spiritual health for us save as we seek in Christ's strength to keep the law, and practice the love of God and neighbor for which it calls.

Suppose people generally began to say: "By God's help I will live by the Ten Commandments every day from now on. I will set myself to honor God and obey him. I will take note of all that he says. I will be in church for worship each week. I will not commit adultery, or indulge myself in lust, or stir up lust in others. I will not steal, nor leave the path of total honesty. I will not lie or cheat. I will not envy or covet." Community life would be transformed, and massive national problems would dissolve overnight. It is something more to pray and work for.

Suppose all churches and congregations were ablaze with zeal for God, and for personal holiness, and for national righteousness—why, that would be revival! Revival is a divine visitation of communities, and its moral force is unrivaled. When God quickens his church, the tremendous purging power that overflows transforms the moral tone of society in a way that nothing else can do. That we need revival is not open to doubt; that this need should drive us to prayer cannot be doubted either.

Where the law's moral absolutes are not respected, people cease to respect either themselves or each other; humanity is deformed, and society slides into the killing decadence of mutual exploitation and self-indulgence. Living in the 1990s, we know all about the disease. It is worth considering what it would be like to be cured. Who knows? We might even be given grace to find the prospect attractive.

1

Blueprint for Behavior

L ife means relationships: with God, men, and things. Get your relationships right, and life is joy, but it is a burden otherwise. It is natural to love life, and against nature to want it to stop; yet today, as when Christianity was born, many experience life as such a meaningless misery that their thoughts turn seriously to suicide. What has gone wrong? Probably relationships. Though depression may have physical roots and yield to physical treatment, disordered relationships are usually at least part of the trouble, and for a full cure these have to be put straight.

What does that involve? Social workers know how lack of meaningful human relations wastes the spirit, and try to bring help at this point. That alone, however, is less than half the remedy. True joy comes only through meaningful relations with God, in tasting his love and walking Christ's way. This is the real *dolce vita*, the life that is genuinely sweet and good.

Forgotten Wisdom

Now the blueprint for this life was set out for all time in the Ten Commandments which God gave the Jews through Moses on Sinai about thirteen centuries before Christ. Yesterday's Christians saw them as (to quote the title of William Barclay's exposition of them) *The Plain Man's Guide to Ethics*. They were right. Today's world, even today's church, has largely forgotten them (could you recite them?). That is our folly and loss. For here, in nugget form, is the wisdom we need.

Because Scripture calls God's Ten Commandments "law" we assume they are like the law of the land, a formal code of dos and don'ts, restricting personal freedom for the sake of public order. But the comparison is wrong. *Torah* (Hebrew for "law") means the sort of instruction a good parent gives his child. Proverbs 1:8 and 6:20 actually use "torah" for parental teaching.

Think of all the wise man's words to his son in Proverbs 1:8-8:36 as addressed to us by our heavenly Father himself (as indeed they are, as in Augustine's true phrase "what thy Scripture says, thou dost say"). That will give you a right idea of the nature and purpose of God's law. It is there, not to thwart self-expression (though it may sometimes feel like that—for children hate discipline!), but to lead us into those ways that are best for us. God's parental law expresses God's parental love.

Sub-Christian?

Some read the Old Testament as so much primitive groping and guesswork, which the New Testament sweeps away. But "God . . . spoke through the prophets" (Hebrews 1:1), of whom Moses was the greatest (see Deuteronomy 34:10-12); and his Commandments, given through Moses, set a moral and spiritual standard for living which is not superseded, but carries God's authority forever. Note that Jesus' twofold law of love, summarizing the Commandments, comes from Moses' own God-taught elaboration of them (for that is what the Pentateuchal law-codes are). "Love your God" is from Deuteronomy 6:5, "love your neighbor" from Leviticus 19:18.

It cannot be too much stressed that Old Testament moral teaching (as distinct from the Old Testament revelation of grace) is not inferior to that of the New Testament, let alone the conventional standards of our time. The barbarities of lawless sex, violence, and exploitation, cutthroat business methods, class warfare, disregard for one's family, and the like are sanctioned only by our modern secular society. The supposedly primitive Old Testament, and the

3000-year-old Commandments in particular, are bulwarks against all these things.

But (you say) doesn't this sort of talk set the Old Testament above Christ? Can that be right? Surely teaching that antedates him by a millennium and a quarter must be inferior to his? Surely the Commandments are too negative, always and only saying "don't . . ."? Surely we must look elsewhere for full Christian standards? Fair queries; but there is a twofold answer.

First, Christ said in the Sermon on the Mount (Matthew 5:17) that he came not to *destroy* the law but to *fulfill* it; that is, to be, and help others to be, all that God in the Commandments had required. What Jesus destroyed was inadequate expositions of the law, not the law itself (Matthew 5:21-48; 15:1-9; etc.). By giving truer expositions, he actually republished the law. The Sermon on the Mount itself consists of themes from the Decalogue developed in a Christian context.

Second, the negative form of the Commandments has positive implications. "Where a sin is forbidden, the contrary duty is commanded" (Westminster Larger Catechism, question 99). The negative form was needed at Sinai (as in the West today) to curb current lawlessness which threatened both godliness and national life. But the positive content pointed up by Christ—loving God with all one's powers, and one's neighbor as oneself—is very clearly there, as we shall see.

Further Bible Study

Christ and the law:
- Matthew 5:17-48; 12:1-14; 15:1-9; 22:34-40
A new life-style for new people:
- Ephesians 4:17-5:14

Questions for Thought and Discussion

- Why are relationships so important in our lives, and where does relationship with God fit in?
- What does Packer mean in saying that Jesus "republished the law"?
- The law takes the form of a series of prohibitions; yet it is held to be positive, not negative, in its content. Explain this.

2

I and You

Of the relationships which make our life, some are personal, some not. A personal relationship is with a personal subject, a "you" who says "I" when addressing us. An impersonal relationship is with a nonpersonal object, a thing, an "it." Our relations with, for instance, cars, houses, ovens, and computers are impersonal, even if we give them pet names; we use them as conveniences, means of expressing ourselves and executing our plans, and rightly so. But to handle persons that way is wrong and indeed destructive, for persons cannot stand being treated as things. Persons have value in themselves and are ends in themselves; they are to be respected as people, not used as pawns.

Putting it positively, persons make claims. They communicate, and ask us to communicate back. In truly personal relations each loves, honors, and serves the other, and response is the rule of life. In this fallen world, where all too often you are your god and I am mine, few relationships, even at home and with so-called friends, are personal enough; we alternately use and ignore each other dreadfully. "Nobody treats me as a person; nobody cares for me" is very much a cry of our time, but the problem is as old as mankind.

Personal Relations with God

Now, the Christian's relationship with God the Creator is a personal, "I-you" affair throughout. To him God is not, as he is to some, a cosmic force to harness, an infinite "it" claiming no more from him than the genie of the lamp did from Aladdin. Christians know that God has called them into a relation of mutual love and service, of mutual listening and response, of asking, giving, taking, and sharing on both sides. Christians learn this from watching and listening to God incarnate in the Gospel stories, and from noting the words of invitation, command, and promise that God spoke through prophets and apostles. And the twice-stated formula of the Commandments (Exodus 20:1-17; Deuteronomy 5:6-21) makes it particularly plain.

For the Commandments are God's edict to persons he has loved and saved, to whom he speaks in "I-you" terms at each point. "I am the Lord your God, who brought you out ... you shall ... " The ten directives, which embody the Creator's intention for human life as such, are here presented as means of maintaining a redeemed relationship already given by grace. And for Christians today, as for the Jews at Sinai, law-keeping (that is, meeting the claims of our God, commandments 1-4, and our neighbor, commandments 5-10) is not an attempt to win God's admiration and put him in our debt, but the form and substance of grateful personal response to his love.

We have been speaking of our Maker as if he were one person, as Jews, Moslems, and Unitarians suppose him to be; but this is the moment to point out that Christians know the one God to be tripersonal, and know too that the fellowship with the Father and the Son through the Spirit into which they, as saved sinners, are called is to be modeled on the Son's fellowship with the Father, as revealed in his life on earth. Loving obedience, joyful loyalty, and wholehearted devotion to his Father was Jesus' way; this same attitude to both the Father and the Son (and indeed the Spirit, save that we do not deal with the Spirit in the same direct manner) must now be ours. Our love-relationship to the persons of the Godhead is thus to be modeled on a love-relationship within the Godhead itself. No personal bond that any man ever knows is deeper or more demanding than this—or (be it added) has more transforming effect.

Into all human relationships that grow, five elements enter on both sides: accepting, asking, promising, pleasing, and where necessary apologizing. Now when God takes us into his family, he accepts us through Christ's atonement; he asks for the service of our lives; his "precious and very great promises" to us (2 Peter 1:4) guarantee that we shall be protected and provided for; and he commits himself to please us by leading us into the fullness of his joy. (No apologies are ever needed for any of that!—it is all great and glorious grace.)

Our part is to accept the triune Jehovah as our God; to ask, and depend on him daily, for whatever we need; to pledge our loyal obedience, and keep our promise in his strength; to aim in all we do at pleasing him; and constantly to practice repentance, which starts with confessing and apologizing for our sins and ends with renouncing them and asking to be delivered from them. As we attend to the wishes of those we love in the human family, so we attend to the law of the Lord out of love for the Lord of the law.

The Pharisees, thinking that they did God service by lovelessly serving the law, depersonalized all relationships and dehumanized themselves, and Jesus damned them for it. Loving relations with God, and with others for his sake, are what his service, as set forth in the Decalogue, is really all about. Love responding to his love, as he declares "I am . . . you shall . . ." is the real secret of law-keeping. Have we learned this secret yet?

Further Bible Study

Law-keeping with love:
- Deuteronomy 11

Law-keeping without love:
- Matthew 23

Questions for Thought and Discussion

- Why is it wrong to use people? Under what circumstances do we do it?
- What is the importance of the "I-you" relationship between God and us in determining our response to the Commandments?
- What does it mean to say that the Pharisees depersonalized relationships and so dehumanized themselves?

3

Law and Love

The Ten Commandments' stock is low today. Why? Partly because they are law, naming particular things that should and should not be done. People dislike law (that is one sign of our sinfulness), and the idea is widespread that Christians should not be led by law, only by love.

Situation Ethics

This idea, for which "situation ethics" is the modern name, sees the Decalogue, with the rest of the Bible's teaching on behavior, as merely a time-honored rule of thumb (not divine teaching, but human generalizing) about ways in which love is ordinarily expressed. But, say situationists, all rules have exceptions, and the Commandments may rightly be overridden if we think we can thereby do more people more good. So in every situation the question is whether law-keeping is really the best we can do. Thus moral life becomes a jam session in which at any time I may improvise for myself rather than play the notes in the score.

Attempts have been made to justify in situationist terms actions ranging from fornication to political subversion, on the grounds of their having been done in a good cause. Situationism says that the end will justify the means.

False Antithesis

But the love-or-law antithesis is false, just as the down-grading of law is perverse. Love and law are not opponents but allies, forming together the axis of true morality. Law needs love as its drive, else we get the Pharisaism that puts principles before people and says one can be perfectly good without actually loving one's neighbor. The truest and kindest way to see situationism is as a reaction against real or imaginary Pharisaism. Even so it is a jump from the frying pan into the fire, inasmuch as correctness, however cold, does less damage than lawlessness, however well-meant. And love needs law as its eyes, for love (Christian *agape* as well as sexual *eros*) is blind. To want to love someone Christianly does not of itself tell you how to do it. Only as we observe the limits set by God's law can we really do people good.

Keep two truths in view. First, God's law expresses his character. It reflects his own behavior; it alerts us to what he will love and hate to see in us. It is a recipe for holiness, consecrated conformity to God, which is his true image in man. And as such (this is the second truth) God's law fits human nature. As cars, being made as they are, only work well with gas in the tank, so we, being made as we are, only find fulfillment in a life of law-keeping. This is what we were both made and redeemed for.

Permissive?

Situationism is worldliness, not only because it opens the door so obviously to wayward self-indulgence, but also because it aims to squeeze Christian morality into the fashionable "permissive" mold of decadent Western secularism, which rejects the restrictions of all external authority and is sure that we are wise and good enough to see what is really best just by looking. But by biblical standards this is one of many delusions born of the satanic, God-defying pride with which we fallen creatures are all infected.

Jesus, God's Son incarnate, was the perfect man, able truly to say, "I love the Father" and "I always do what is pleasing to him" (John 14:31; 8:29). If anyone was qualified to detect shortcomings in the Ten Commandments and lead us beyond them to something better, it was he. But what did he do? He affirmed them as having authority forever (Matthew 5:18-20) and as central to true religion (19:17-19). He expounded them, showing how they forbade wrong attitudes as well as wrong actions and nailing evasions (5:21-30, sixth and seventh commandments; 15:3-9, fifth commandment; cf. 23:16-22; 5:33-36, on the principle of the third commandment). And he made a point of insisting that he kept them (Luke 6:6-10, fourth commandment). When John says, "This is the love of God, that we keep his commandments" (1 John 5:3), his words describe Jesus' own religion, as well as reminding us that Jesus defined love and discipleship to himself in terms of keeping his own commands (John 14:15, 21-24; cf. Matthew 28:19, 20). Commandment-keeping is the only true way to love the Father and the Son.

And it is the only true way to love one's neighbor, too. When Paul says that "he who loves his neighbor has fulfilled the law" (Romans 13:8; cf. 10), he explains himself by showing that love to neighbor embraces the specific prohibitions of adultery, murder, stealing, and envy. He does not say that love to neighbor cancels them! When my neighbor, echoing the pop song, says "Come on, let's sleep together," or sin together some other way, I show love to him (or her) not by consenting, but by resisting and showing why the suggestion should be withdrawn, as Joseph did (Genesis 39:8).

Moral permissiveness, supposedly so liberating and fulfilling, is actually wounding and destructive: not only of society (which God's law protects), but also of the lawless individual, who gets coarsened and reduced as a person every time. The first advocate of permissiveness was Satan at the Fall, but his promise of Godlikeness to the lawless was a lie. The Christian's most loving service to his neighbor in our modern world, which so readily swallows this ancient lie, is to uphold the authority of God's law as man's one true guide to true life.

Further Bible Study

Love and commandments:
- 1 John 2, 3
- Galatians 5:2-6:10

Questions for Thought and Discussion

- How do situationists justify actions which others think wrong? Do you agree with their reasoning? Can you refute it?
- "Love and law are not opponents but allies." In what way?
- What does God's law reveal about human nature? What help is this to us?

4

The Lord Your God

When God gave Israel the Commandments on Sinai (Exodus 20:1-17), he introduced them by introducing himself. "God spoke all these words, saying, 'I am the LORD your God, who brought you out of . . . bondage. You shall . . .'" (verse 1ff.). What God is and has done determines what his people must be and do. So study of the Decalogue should start by seeing what it tells us about God.

First, he is the God of creation and covenant. The fourth commandment says that he made heaven, earth, sea, "and all that is in them" (verse 11). You and I and everything else exist, then, not independently, but by God's will and power. With this, the five-times-repeated formula, "the LORD (Yahweh) your God" (verses 2, 5, 7, 10, 12) reveals a covenant commitment.

"The LORD" is "Yahweh" (Jehovah), the proper name by which God wanted the Israelites to know him (see 3:15). It is from the verb "to be." God's explanation of it can be rendered "I am what (or who) I am" or "I will be what I will be" (3:13ff.), but in either case it highlights his self-existence, eternity, and sovereignty. The added words "your God," however, point to a special relationship for which "covenant" is the regular biblical term.

Covenant

"Yahweh" is God's covenant name, and Scripture compares his covenant to the man's commitment in marriage: a free, deliberate undertaking to love, protect, and provide for the one whom he calls "my wife" and to whom he presents himself as "your husband." "Your Maker is your husband" (Isaiah 54:5). There is no richer declaration of God's love-link with the redeemed than the simple phrase "your God," with others equally simple: "God to you" (Genesis 17:7); "I am with you" (Haggai 1:13; so said Jesus, Matthew 28:20); "God is for us" (Romans 8:31). Prepositions and personal pronouns can say a lot!

Creation and covenant together give God a double claim on our obedience. The claim springs, you might say, from both paternity (fatherhood in the sense of creatorship) and matrimony (the covenant relationship). The Creator's covenant, which in Old Testament times was for Abraham's seed through Isaac and Jacob, now embraces all who are Abraham's seed through Christ, by faith. So all we who trust Jesus Christ as our Savior must realize that, according to the covenant which Jesus mediates, God stands pledged to bless us "in Christ with every spiritual blessing" (Ephesians 1:3; cf. Romans 8:32); and obedient faithfulness to him, as our Father through Christ and our Husband in the covenant, must henceforth be the rule of our lives.

Liberty

Second, God is *redeemer* and *rewarder*. Redeeming means recovering from alien possession, normally by payment (thus, the old-style pawnbroker displayed with his three brass balls the sign "Redemption Office"). The God who redeemed Jews from Egyptian slavery has redeemed Christians from bondage to sin and Satan at the cost of Calvary. Now it is by keeping his law that the liberty thus secured is to be preserved.

This was true for Israel at a typical level: God told them that obedience would mean, instead of captivity, long life in "the land which the LORD your God gives you" (verse 12), as he showed "steadfast love to thousands" of those who loved him and kept his commands (verse 6). But for Israel then, as for Christians now, the deeper truth was this: that keeping God's law brings that deeper freedom (inner contentment) at which the tenth commandment tells us to aim. That is why James called it "the law of liberty" (James 1:25). Law-keeping is that life for which we were fitted by nature, unfitted by sin, and refitted by grace, the life God loves to see and reward; and for that life *liberty* is the proper name.

Jealousy

Third, God is *jealous*, and *judges*. His jealousy is not a moral flaw, as the word might suggest, but a moral excellence; it is the jealousy of a loyal husband who rightly desires his wife's exclusive affection. Where God's love is spurned, his will flouted, and his loyalty betrayed, he can be expected to "visit" as judge (verse 5). God speaks of those whom he thus visits as persons who, in each successive generation, "hate" him, and the verb points to the fact that deep down all who defy God's rule without being able to forget his reality do wish him dead, or different, and resent with bitter irreverence both his claims and his warnings. Can we wonder, then, or demur, when God deals with such folk in retributive judgment?

Do we reckon with God the lawgiver as he really is? "Note then the kindness and the severity of God," says Paul in Romans 11:22, speaking of the gospel; "severity towards those who have fallen, but God's kindness to you, provided you continue in his kindness . . ." Kindness and severity appear together in the Decalogue too, and we shall be wise to heed its witness to both.

Further Bible Study

Covenant and commandment:
- Deuteronomy 29, 30

Questions for Thought and Discussion

- Why should study of the Decalogue start by examining what it says about God?
- What does marriage teach us about God's covenant commitment to his people?
- How does keeping God's law produce liberty?

5

Who Comes First?

The fundamental commandment, first in importance as well as in order, and basic to every other, is, "You shall have no other gods before me." True religion starts with accepting this as one's rule of life.

Loyalty

Your god is what you love, seek, worship, serve, and allow to control you. Paul calls covetousness "idolatry" (Colossians 3:5) because what you covet—houses, possessions, ornaments, money, status, success, or whatever—is "had" as a god in this sense. To have your Maker and Savior as your God in preference to any other object of devotion (which is the point of "before") means that you live for him as his person in faithful and loyal obedience. The attitude of devoted loyalty to God, expressed in worship and service according to his Word, is that fear of the Lord (reverence, not panic!) which the Bible sees as the beginning and indeed the essence of wisdom (Job 28:28; Psalm 111:10; Proverbs 1:7, 9:10). Heart-loyalty is the soil out of which holy living grows.

Other Gods

What other gods could one "have" beside the Lord? Plenty. For Israel there were the Canaanite Baals, those jolly nature-gods whose worship, as we know from archaeology and Scriptures like Hosea 4:11-14, was a rampage of gluttony, drunkenness, and ritual prostitution. For us there are still the great gods Sex, Shekels, and Stomach (an unholy trinity constituting one god, self), and the other enslaving trio, Pleasure, Possessions, and Position, whose worship is described in 1 John 2:16 as "the lust of the flesh and lust of the eyes and the pride of life." Football, the Firm, Freemasonry, the Family are also gods for some, and indeed the list of other gods is endless, for anything that anyone allows to run his life becomes his god, and the claimants for this prerogative are legion. In the matter of life's basic loyalty, temptation is a many-headed monster.

Concentrated Living

The great commandment, the first one, said Jesus, is to love the Lord your God with *all* your heart and *all* your soul and *all* your mind (Matthew 22:37; the version of these words in Mark 12:30 adds a further dimension, "all your strength"). Quoted from Deuteronomy 6:4ff., where it is introduced with a reminder that the Lord is "one," meaning "the only one" (the point being, first, that none of the other gods around may be identified with him, and second, that being the only proper claimant of our worship and service he may rightly ask for it all), this saying shows us what loyalty to God requires. It calls for love, responding to God's love in making and saving you; and it demands total concentration of purpose, so that in everything you do there is just one thing you aim at—pleasing and glorifying the Lord.

"No soldier on service gets entangled in civilian pursuits," wrote Paul, "since his aim is to satisfy the one who enlisted him" (2 Timothy 2:4). In business too, employers expect the undivided loyalty of their staff, and we think them entitled to do so. But how much stronger is God's claim! Do we give our God the resolute, wholehearted allegiance for which he asks, and which is his due? Does he really come first in our lives?

What will it mean in practice for me to put God first? This much, at least. All the 101 things I have to do each day, and the 101 demands on me which I know I must try to meet, will all be approached as ventures of loving service to him, and I shall do the best I can in everything for his sake—which attitude, as George

Herbert quaintly said, "makes drudgery divine; who sweeps a room, as for thy laws, makes that and th' action fine."

And then I shall find that, through the secret work of the Spirit which is known by its effects, my very purpose of pleasing God gives me new energy for all these tasks and relationships, energy which otherwise I could not have had. "I could not love thee, dear, so much loved I not honor more," said the poet. Put "God" for "honor," and you have the deepest truth about the Christian's love of his neighbor. Self-absorbed resentments dissolve, and zest for life, happiness in doing things, and love for others all grow great when God comes first.

So wake up, enthrone your God—and *live*!

Further Bible Study

Wrong priorities:
● Haggai 1
God despised, wearied, and robbed:
● Malachi 1-4

Questions for Thought and Discussion

● What characterized whomever or whatever a person chooses for his god? What god (or God) do you serve?
● Why would one say, "Heart-loyalty is the soil out of which holy living grows"?
● What does it mean in practice to have no other gods before God?

6

Imagination

popular song in my youth began, "Imagination is funny; it makes a cloudy day sunny . . ." Imagination is amazing! Imagination creates (think of *Lord of the Rings*, or a Shakespeare play, or a Beethoven symphony). It upholds relationships, for it shows you what the other person thinks and feels. As part of God's image in us, it is good and essential; persons without imagination are badly lacking. But, like all good things, imagination can go bad. It can be used for withdrawing from reality into fantasy, and that is wrong and ruinous. Children love make-believe, but adult relationships need realism. If one imagines other people to be different from what they are, there will be trouble, as psychiatrists and marriage counselors know all too well. And what is true of human relationships is truer still of our relationship with God.

Imagining God

How should we form thoughts of God? Not only can we not imagine him adequately, since he is at every point greater than we can grasp; we dare not trust anything our imagination suggests about him, for the built-in habit of fallen minds is to scale God down. Sin began as response to the temptation, "You will be like God" (Genesis 3:5), and the effect of our wanting to be on God's level is that we bring him down to ours. This is unrealistic, not to say irreverent, but it is what we all do when imagination is in the saddle.

Hence the second commandment, "You shall not make for yourself a graven image, or any likeness of anything." This forbids, not worshipping many gods (the first commandment covered that), but imagining the true God as like yourself or something lower. God's real attack is on mental images, of which metal images are more truly the consequence than the cause. When Israelites worshipped God under the form of a golden bull-calf, they were using their imagination to conceive him in terms of power without purity; this was their basic sin. And if imagination leads our thoughts about God, we too shall go astray. No statement starting, "This is how I like to think of God" should ever be trusted. An imagined God will always be more or less imaginary and unreal.

The Real God

Is it not maddening when, after correcting someone's wrong ideas, you find that he was not listening, and is still trotting out his old mistake? Measure by this the provocation offered to God if we fail to take note of what he has shown us of himself. For he has made a point of showing us both his hand and his heart, in his words and deeds recorded in Scripture, and supremely in the earthly life of his incarnate Son, Jesus Christ, who is in every sense his image (Colossians 1:15; cf. Hebrews 1:3; John 14:7-10). God the Father is altogether Jesus-like!—it is the most breathtaking news that anyone can ever hear. But do we attend to what is revealed? I fear not. Imagination takes over again.

What do we do? We *imagine* a clash between the presentations of God in different parts of the Old Testament, and between the entire Old Testament presentation and what we *imagine* Jesus to have been. What sort of person do you think of him as? Gentle, meek, and mild? Kind, and endlessly ready to be entreated and forgive? True—but only half the truth, and a half-truth treated as the whole truth becomes a whole falsehood. Have you forgotten how he whipped tradesmen out of the temple (Mark 11:15-17; John 2:14-16), and threw verbal vitriol at recognized church leaders (Matthew 23, etc.), and cursed the fig tree as a sign of judgment to come on unfaithful Israel (Mark 11:12-14, 20ff.)? In Jesus, as in all God's self-disclosure throughout the Bible, there is a combination of pity with purity, passion with power, and slowness to anger with severity of judgment, that should humble us to the roots of our being and move us every day to cry for mercy. But are we realists enough to see this? Or has our imagination betrayed us once again?

Do we like to think that God is light as well as love (1 John 1:5; 4:8), great and terrible as well as steadfast in love (Nehemiah 1:5)? Maybe not, but this is how he is, and woe betide us if we are foolish and inattentive enough to imagine him different.

God ends the second commandment (Exodus 20:5ff.) by reminding us of his real nature as the *jealous* God who seeks total loyalty, the *just* God who judges his foes as they deserve, and the *gracious* God who shows "steadfast love to thousands (of generations) of those who love him and keep his commandments." And how should we keep this one? By reining in our disordered imaginations and reverently accepting that God is as he says he is. How unready and slow we are to do that! Yet we must learn to do it; for it is only as rose-colored fantasy is abandoned, and realism takes its place, that true worship—worship, that is, in truth—can begin.

Further Bible Study

The golden bull-calf, and what God thought of it:
- Exodus 32

Questions for Thought and Discussion

- Why cannot human imagination adequately picture God?
- What is the real sin that prompts the making of images of God? Is this sin a problem in your life? What will you do about it if so?
- In your own words, what is God like?

7

Are You Serious?

"The purpose of words," said a cynical diplomat, I forget who, "is to conceal thought." As a comment on how we actually talk, this statement is too true to be good. Regularly we talk for effect, saying to each other things we do not mean and could not defend, and giving assurances which we have no firm purpose to fulfill. "Are you serious?" is a question that often needs asking, for often when we should be speaking seriously, we are not.

Reluctance to treat our word as our bond—unwillingness, that is, to count ourselves committed by what we actually said—is a symptom of sin, which is the moral maggot destroying integrity. Why are marriage vows, contracts between employer and employee, and ordinary promises—to do this, to see to that, to be here, to go there—so frequently broken? Why is our life littered with promises which, whether from malice, bad management, self-seeking, or sheer carelessness, we have failed to keep? Why do we so often let down those who trusted what we said? Because of our sinful unwillingness to take our own words seriously.

Taking God's Name in Vain

The Bible, however, takes promises very seriously; God demands full faithfulness of our vows. Why? Partly because trustworthiness is part of his image, which he wants to see in us; partly because without it society falls apart. The third commandment highlights God's concern at this point.

"You shall not take the name of the Lord your God in vain," it says. "In vain" means "for unreality." What is forbidden is any use or involvement of God's name that is empty, frivolous, or insincere. This touches three things at least.

The first thing is *irreverence*, speaking or thinking of God in a way that insults him by not taking seriously his wisdom and goodness. Job offered sacrifices on behalf of his children while they were alive, for fear that they had "cursed God in their hearts" (Job 1:5); and after their deaths when his wife in her bitterness urged him, "Curse God, and die" (2:9), he would not do it. Whenever sinful self-absorption makes us hate God for what he allows to happen to us or others, we break the third commandment.

The second thing is *bad language*, using God's holy name as a swear-word to voice men's unholy feelings. Everyday profanity— for example, "Oh God," "Oh Christ," and the rest—may not be the worst of sins, but it is a nasty breach of the third commandment, since it expresses neither faith nor worship. Rage overcomes us all sometimes, and it is better, no doubt, at such times to speak violently and blasphemously than to act violently and go berserk. But if you dwell often on the truth that God is Lord and orders everything, even the frustrations, for our sanctification (Hebrews 12:5-11; cf. Romans 8:28ff.), you will find yourself able increasingly, even in the most maddening moments, to "keep your cool"—and that is best of all.

The third thing, and the one which needs special stress because, as we saw, we are all so slack here, is *promise-keeping*. If we have invoked God by name in order to give our words credence, it is monstrous irreverence if we then go back on them. "You shall not swear by my name falsely, and so profane the name of your God" (Leviticus 19:12; cf. Jeremiah 5:2; Zechariah 5:4). The Lord will not hold him guiltless who takes his name in vain.

And the point goes deeper. When Jesus attacked the Pharisees' idea that one can break without guilt any oath sworn by any sacred object, so long as God's name has not been explicitly mentioned, his point was that you cannot keep God out of any transaction; he is everywhere, and all promises are made in his presence and involve him, whether his name is mentioned or not (Matthew 5:33ff.). So all promises are sacred, and must be kept. Children know this, and feel it very strongly; it is tragic that adults should so often forget it.

The godly man, therefore, will make promises cautiously but keep them conscientiously once they are made, knowing that irresponsibility and unreliability here are great and grievous sins. How hard we find this to learn! And how much we need to learn it!

Further Bible Study

Why words need watching:
- Matthew 12:22-37

Questions for Thought and Discussion

- Why does God demand that we keep our vows?
- Does taking the Lord's name in vain have to do only with promises made in his name? Why or why not?
- How would you refute the Pharisees' claim that oaths not specifically using God's name may be broken without guilt?

8

Take My Time

The fourth commandment, "Remember the sabbath day, to keep it holy," raises questions. First, the *historical* problem: was there sabbath observance before Sinai? The word "remember" introducing the command, plus the narrative of God's earlier non-provision of manna on the seventh day because he had given it as a sabbath for rest (Exodus 16:22-30), suggests that there was, while Genesis 2:2ff. (God blessed the seventh day and hallowed it, because on it God rested) takes sabbath-keeping back to creation itself.

Sabbath & Lord's Day

Second, the *dispensational* problem: what is the relation between the Old Testament sabbath, the seventh day of the week, commemorating creation and redemption from Egypt (Deuteronomy 5:15), and the "Lord's day" when Christians met for worship, the first day of the week, commemorating Jesus' resurrection (see John 20:19; Acts 20:7; Revelation 1:10)? For Thomas Aquinas and the Westminster Confession, the relation is just a new way of counting six-and-one, so that Lord's day observance is the Christian form of sabbath-keeping. "From the beginning of the world to the resurrection of Christ, God appointed the seventh day of the week to be a weekly Sabbath; and the first day of the week ever since . . . which is the Christian Sabbath" (Westminster Shorter Catechism).

This seems the natural reading of the scanty evidence (i.e., the three New Testament texts noted above); but Seventh-Day Adventists continue the Saturday sabbath, denying that a change has been made, while many, with Augustine, seeing that the commanded "rest" was typical of our rest of faith in Christ, conclude that, like other Old Testament types, this commandment is now abolished. Then their reason for keeping the Lord's day is the church's traditional practice rather than God's direct command.

Third, the *ethical* problem: if the Lord's day is the Christian sabbath, how do we keep it holy? Answer—by behaving as Jesus did. His sabbaths were days, not for idle amusement, but for worshiping God and doing good—what the Shorter Catechism calls "works of necessity and mercy" (see Luke 4:16; 13:10-17; 14:1-6). Freedom from secular chores secures freedom to serve the Lord on his own day. Matthew Henry says that the sabbath was made a day of holy *rest* so that it might be a day of holy *work*. From this holy work, in our sedentary and lonely world, physical recreation and family fun will not be excluded, but worship and Christian fellowship will come first.

Your Time is God's

Inferences from these three questions may be disputable, but the underlying principle is clear—namely, that we must honor God not only by our loyalty (first commandment) and thought-life (second commandment) and words (third commandment), but also by our use of time, in a rhythm of toil and rest; six days for work crowned by one day for worship. God's claim on our sabbaths reminds us that all our time is his gift, to be given back to him and used for him. "Take my life" includes "take my moments and my days—take my time, all of it." This is where true obedience to the fourth commandment begins.

That Christians are stewards of the gifts and money that God gives them is a familiar truth nowadays; that we are stewards of the time we are given is less stressed, but just as true. We can learn this from the Puritans, who often voiced their sense of the preciousness of time, and from Paul, who urges, "Look carefully then how you walk, . . . making the most of the time, because the days are evil" (Ephesians 5:15ff.; cf. Colossians 4:5). "Time" means "moment" or "opportunity"; "making the most of" is literally "buying up," "redeeming from waste or uselessness"; and the days are still "evil" in Paul's sense, namely full of temptation and opposition from satanic sources (cf. 6:11-17). Satan wants to see every minute misused; it is for us to make every minute count for God.

How? Not by a frenzied rushing to pack a quart of activity into a pint pot of time (a common present-day error), but by an ordered life-style in which, within the set rhythm of toil and rest, work and worship, due time is allotted to sleep, family, wage-earning, homemaking, prayer, recreation, and so on, so that we master time instead of being mastered by it.

Few of us, perhaps, take the fourth commandment as seriously as we should. My own failures here have been great. What, I wonder, about you?

Further Bible Study

How to give time to God:
- Isaiah 58

Questions for Thought and Discussion

- What relation do you see between the Old Testament sabbath and the New Testament Lord's day? Defend your view against alternative views.
- How can we keep the sabbath holy in our time?
- Practically speaking, what is involved in giving all our time to God?

9

God and the Family

After four commandments about God's direct claims come six on duty toward others. The first of these is, "Honor your father and your mother".

Respect for Parents

Scripture stresses the responsibility of parents to train their children, and children to honor their parents. In the Old Testament, disrespect for parents was a major sin: one who cursed a parent could be executed (Exodus 21:17; Leviticus 20:9), and Ham was punished for mocking his father Noah as the latter slept off the effects of potent homemade wine (Genesis 9:20-27). In the New Testament, Jesus flays the Pharisees for claiming to keep the fifth commandment while actually breaking it by leaving parents destitute (Matthew 15:3-9), and disobedience to parents betokens decadence and apostasy (Romans 1:30; 2 Timothy 3:2).

Why does God highlight the duty to "love, honour, and succour my father and mother" (as the Catechism puts it)? For many reasons.

First, the family is the basic social unit; no nation is stable or virile where family life is weak.

Second, the family is the basic spiritual unit, in which God makes parents their children's pastors and teachers.

Third, children do in fact owe their parents a huge debt of gratitude for years of care and provision.

Fourth, children need parental guidance more than they know, and impoverish themselves by rejecting it. The long life promised in Exodus 20:12 and Deuteronomy 5:16 to those who honor their parents is not guaranteed to any Christian, but it remains true that children who flout their parents suffer loss. They forfeit a degree of human maturity, and make it harder for themselves to honor a Father in heaven.

Fifth, in pre-social security days the aged had only their own children to provide for them; and even in the welfare state aging parents need their children's loving concern, just as the children once needed their parents' care.

God and Families

None of this, of course, justifies parental tyrannizing or possessiveness, or requires children to bow to either. "Do not exasperate your children [and you] must not goad your children to resentment, but give them the instruction, and the correction, which belong to a Christian upbringing" (Colossians 3:21; Ephesians 6:4, NEB). Should one's parents impede one's discipleship, disobedience to parents would become a necessary evil.

But what we must realize is that God, who is himself a father—Father of our Lord Jesus Christ, and of all Christians through him—cares about families enormously. Family life, with its built-in responsibilities for both parents and children, is part of his purpose for all, and the way we behave as children and parents is a prime test of both our humanity and our godliness. Love—the caring love of parents who respect their children and want to see them mature, and the grateful love of children who respect their parents and want to see them content—is our great need here.

How urgent it is in these days that parents and children together should relearn the ways of Christian family life. In the West, yesterday's extended family has shrunk to today's nuclear family; social security and community affluence have reduced the family's importance as an economic unit; and all this has weakened family relationships. Parents are too busy to give time to their children, and young people, identifying with current "youth" culture, are more prone than ever to write off their parents as clueless old fuddy-dud-dies. But the fifth commandment recalls us to God's order at this point.

Honestly, now: what is, or has been, your attitude to your parents? *Honoring* them means respecting them, so to speak, for their office, their relationship to you, as we should respect clergymen and public officials, whatever we think of their personal limitations or private lives. A school contemporary of mine carved out a brilliant academic career, but grew ashamed of his parents (his father was a baker), and would not visit them or let them visit him. As in a pre-pension age the Pharisees let folk duck out of financial responsibility for parents (Jesus savaged them for it: see Mark 7:6-13), so people today duck the task of caring for parents who can no longer care for themselves. But none may claim to love their neighbor while they shrug off their parents. Some of us have some repenting to do.

Further Bible Study

Pattern for families:
• Colossians 3:18-21 (cf. Ephesians 5:21-6:4)
How Jesus honored his mother:
• John 2:1-11; 19:25-27

Questions for Thought and Discussion

• Why can't a nation be strong if family life in it is weak?
• How is knowledge of God's fatherhood a help to parents?
• In what way is the home a testing-ground?

10

Life Is Sacred

The sixth commandment (Exodus 20:13; Deuteronomy 5:17) is "you shall not kill" (RSV) or "murder" (RV, NEB). The word signifies malicious and unlawful killing, so "murder" is more accurate. Judicial execution (e.g., for murder) and killing in war are not in view; God actually calls for both in the very books from which the commandment comes (see Exodus 21:12-17; Deuteronomy 20:10-18). However strongly we may think the death penalty inadvisable and even hateful (views vary), we may not invoke this commandment to prove our point; in its context, it has no bearing on either question, but deals with private morality.

Man in God's Image

The commandment rests on the principle that human life is holy, first because it is God's gift and second because man bears God's image (Genesis 1:27; 9:6). Human life is thus the most precious and sacred thing in the world, and to end it, or direct its ending, is God's prerogative alone. We honor God by respecting his image in each other, which means consistently preserving life and furthering each other's welfare in all possible ways.

There are several things, not always called murder, which the commandment rules out. First is *malice*, the desire to diminish someone or, as we say, to "see him dead." Jesus underlined this. "Anyone who nurses anger against his brother must be brought to judgment . . . if he sneers at him he will have to answer for it in the fires of hell" (Matthew 5:22, NEB). Hate in the heart can be as much murder as violence against the person.

Second, the commandment rules out all *cruelty* or *violence* that could weaken or shorten another person's life. It is grievous to see how crimes against the person (mugging and bombing, for instance) have increased in supposedly Christian countries, while brainwashing and interrogation by torture (and sometimes torture without the interrogation) have established themselves as standard resources of modern militarism. Had the sixth commandment been pondered, none of this would be.

Killing the Fetus

Third, the commandment rules out *abortion* because, as genetic science shows, the fetus is from the moment of conception a human being in process (we might say) of arriving. The fact that for several months it cannot survive outside the womb does not affect its right to the same protection that other human beings merit, and which it will itself merit after birth. Abortion can only ever be justified (and then only as a necessary evil) when the pregnancy genuinely endangers the mother's life—and, as doctors know, there are few such cases today. Legalizing abortion on other grounds is a social evil, whatever arguments of convenience are invoked.

Fourth, the commandment rules out *suicide* and *euthanasia*. Suicide (self-murder) is the act of a mind unhinged; though such acts do not of themselves forfeit God's grace, as was once thought, yet suicide is a direct breach of God's command. So is euthanasia, which is either suicide by remote control or murder based on the idea that we may lawfully "put people out of their misery" just as we lawfully shoot horses or get vets to put pets to sleep. But we may not bracket a human being with horses or pets, even if he himself in a pain-maddened moment asks us to. It is good that the law treats both suicide and euthanasia as illegal acts.

(Letting the body die when no hope of recovering consciousness remains is not, of course, euthanasia; in that case, the person must be regarded as in the most important sense dead already. The difficulty in these cases is to judge when the point at which consciousness cannot return has been reached.)

The killing of millions of Jews and cripples by the Nazis, and of millions of Russians by Russian Communists in this century shows whither denial of the sanctity of human life leads. The sixth commandment points the truer and better way.

Murderers

As murder storywriters assume, and as most of us learn in experience, we have in us capacies for fury, fear, envy, greed, conceit, callousness, and hate which, given the right provocation, could make killers out of us all—baby-batterers or Bluebeards, professionsl thugs or amateur hit men. G. K. Chesterton's Father Brown explained his method of detection by saying, "You see, it was I who killed all those people"—in the sense that he looked within himself to find the mentality that would produce the crime he was investigating, and did in fact discover it there. Chesterton lets him moralize:

"No man's really any good till he knows how bad he is, or might be; till he's realized exactly how much right he has to all this snobbery, and sneering, and talking about 'criminals,' as if they were apes in a forest ten thousand miles away . . . till he's squeezed out of his soul the last drop of the oil of the Pharisees; till his only hope is somehow or other to have captured one criminal, and kept him safe and sane under his own hat."

Brown, though fictitious, states fact. When the fathomless wells of rage and hatred in the normal human heart are tapped, the results are fearful. "There but for the grace of God go I." Only restraining and renewing grace enables anyone to keep the sixth commandment.

Further Bible Study

Murder is evil:
- Genesis 4:1-16; 9:1-7

Questions for Thought and Discussion

- Why should hate be bracketed with murder? How do you cope with feelings of fury and hatred against other persons?
- Do you agree with the position stated in this chapter on abortion and euthanasia? Why or why not?
- What is the "truer and better way" that is referred to?

11

Sex Is Sacred

When I was very young and first met the text of the seventh commandment, I thought (believe it or not) that adultery meant simply a grown-up way of behaving. Since then I, like you, have learned that some adults do in fact see sex outside marriage as a sign of being truly grown-up—"mature" is the word used, though I think it is misapplied. (When a Sunday school pupil defined adultery as the sin of pretending to be older than you are, in moral if not physical terms, it seems to me he hit the nail on the head with a resonant bang!) But what the words "you shall not commit adultery" call us to face is, first, that sex is for marriage, and for marriage only; second, that marriage must be seen as a relation of lifelong fidelity; third, that other people's marriages must not be interfered with by sexual intrusion. One mark of true maturity is to grasp these principles, and live by them.

The Place for Sex

Not that Scripture is squeamish about sexual joy, as Christians have sometimes been. Passages like Proverbs 5:18ff. and the Song of Songs show that God, who invented it, is all for it—in its place! But sexual activity is often out of place—when, for instance, it is directed by such motives as the quest for kicks, or for relief from mental or physical tension, or loneliness or boredom, or the desire to control or humiliate; or mere animal reaction to someone's sex appeal. Such motives cheapen sex, making it (despite the short-term excitement) trivial and ugly, and leaving behind, once the thrill is over, more of disgust than delight.

What then is the place and purpose of sex? God intends, as the story of Eve's creation from Adam shows, that the "one flesh" experience should be an expression and a heightening of the partners' sense that, being given to each other, they now belong together, each needing the other for completion and wholeness (see Genesis 2:18-24). This is the "love" that committed couples are to "make" when they mate. Children are born from their relationship, but this is secondary; what is basic is the enriching of their relationship itself through their repeated "knowing" of each other as persons who belong to each other exclusively and without reserve. So the place for sex is the place of lifelong mutual fidelity, i.e. marriage, where sexual experience grows richer as the couple experiences more and more of each other's loving faithfulness in the total relationship.

False Trails

It follows that casual sex outside marriage (called "adultery" if either partner is married, "fornication" if not) cannot fulfill God's ideal, for it lacks the context of pledged fidelity. In casual sex a man does not strictly *love* a woman, but *uses* and so *abuses* her (however willing she may be). Nor can solitary masturbation fulfill God's ideal; sex is for relationships, not ego trips.

And the relationships intended are heterosexual only; God forbids and condemns homosexual practices (Leviticus 18:22; Romans 1:26ff.). In these days it needs to be said, indeed shouted, that accepting as from God a life without what Kinsey called "outlets" (i.e., physical sex acts) does one no harm, nor does it necessarily shrink one's humanity. After all, Jesus, the perfect man, was a celibate, and Paul, whether bereaved, deserted, or never married, lived single throughout his ministry. Not all who wish for a sexual partner can have one, but what God by circumstances calls us to he will also enable us for.

Sex is a Signpost

In the jungle of modern permissiveness the meaning and purpose of sex is missed, and its glory is lost. Our benighted society urgently needs recalling to the noble and ennobling view of sex which Scripture implies and the seventh commandment assumes: namely, that sex is for fully and permanently committed relationships which, by being the blend of affection, loyalty, and biology that they are, prepare us for and help us into that which is their archetype— "the happiness of being freely, voluntarily united" to God, men, and angels "in an ecstasy of love and delight compared with which the most rapturous love between a man and a woman on this earth is mere milk and water" (C. S. Lewis).

Will that be fun? Yes, that is one thing it will be, so no wonder God has made its earthly analogue fun too. Nor may you despise it, any more than you may deify it, on that account. The sweetness of affection between the sexes, linked (as it always is) with the sense that a couple's relationship, however complete, is never quite complete, is actually a jeweled signpost pointing us on to God. When folk in the Romeo-and-Juliet state of mind say "this thing is bigger than us," they speak more truly than they sometimes realize. But a signpost only helps those who will head the way it directs, and if you insisted on camping for life beside a lovely signpost, you would be daft; you would never get anywhere.

Further Bible Study

Sex mishandled:
- Proverbs 6:20-7:27
- 1 Corinthians 6:9-20

The joy of sexual love:
- Song of Solomon 1-8

Questions for Thought and Discussion

- What is the biblical concept of marriage? What does sex outside marriage lack in terms of God's ideal?
- What is God's primary purpose for sex? What does the expression "one flesh" indicate about this?
- How would you counsel a person who confessed to homosexual inclinations?

12

Stop, Thief!

Next to your own persons and your wife, your worldly goods stand closest to you, and God means them to be secured to you, and therefore commands that no one shall take away or lessen any part of his neighbor's possessions . . . Now this is a very common vice . . . For . . . stealing signifies not only emptying chests and pockets, but also taking advantage of others at market, warehouses, wine and beer shops, workshops, in short, wherever men transact business and give money for goods and labor."

So Luther starts expounding the eighth commandment, focusing on the principle of equity involved. Love to our neighbor requires us to hold sacred not only his person (sixth commandment) and his marriage (seventh commandment), but also his *property* and his *due*.

Property

Behind the commandment lies the Bible view of property; namely, that ownership is stewardship. By human law, my property is that which I own and may dispose of as I wish, as distinct from that which I am merely allowed to use as borrower or trustee, under conditions which the owner imposes. Bible-believers, however, know that what human law says I own—my money, goods, legal rights, and titles—I actually hold as God's trustee. In the terms of Jesus' parable, these things are *talents*, lent me by my Lord on a temporary basis to use for him. One day I shall be asked to give account of how I managed those of his resources of which I was given control.

Temptations to steal property—that is, to deprive another person of what he or she has a right to—arise because fallen man always, instinctively, wants more than he has at present, and more than others have. Blind competitiveness, expressing an equally blind jealousy, was the essence of the devil's pride when he rebelled against God, and of Cain's pride when he killed Abel (Genesis 4:4-8), and of Rebekah's and Jacob's pride when they stole Esau's birthright (Genesis 27); and it is the essence of the discontented greed condemned in the tenth commandment, which is itself the cause of the dishonest grabbing forbidden in the eighth. But it is not God's will for us to have anything that we cannot obtain by honorable means, and the only right attitude to others' property is scrupulous concern that ownership be fully respected.

Ways of Thieving

No doubt this principle is both clear and commonplace. After all, every law-code everywhere has always protected property, condemned stealing, and required damages—restitution—in the way that Scripture does (cf. Numbers 5:7; Proverbs 6:30ff.). How else could there ever be ordered community life? It might seem that nothing here needs a second thought.

But wait. How does the principle apply? It reaches further than perhaps we realize.

There is, for instance, theft of *time*, perhaps the commonest form of theft today. Employees contract to do so many hours' work for so much pay, and fail to do it. We start late, finish early, stretch coffee, lunch, and tea breaks, and waste time in between. This is theft.

It is theft too when a tradesman fails to give *value for money*. The Old Testament damns false weights and measures (Deuteronomy 25:13-15; Amos 8:5); the modern equivalent is overpricing goods and services, cashing in on another's need. Profiteering and all forms of overcharging are theft.

Again, it is theft when *debts* are left unpaid, thus robbing the person owed of the use of money to which he is morally entitled. Letting debts hang on is a way of life for some, but Scripture condemns it. "Owe no one anything, except to love one another," says Paul (Romans 13:8). If we really love our neighbor, we shall not try to postpone paying him.

Finally, it is theft to steal a *reputation*, destroying someone's credit by malicious gossip behind his back. "Who steals my purse, steals trash," wrote Shakespeare, "but he that filches from me my good name . . . makes me poor indeed." Thus, gossip is a breach of the ninth commandment; its effect will be a breach of the eighth.

Perhaps we thought that the words "thou shalt not steal" had no relevance for us in our respectability. Perhaps we need to think again. "Let the thief no longer steal," wrote Paul (Ephesians 4:28). Could "Stop, thief!" be a word that God is speaking to you and me?

Restitution

Now be honest. We have been stirring up thoughts about ways of stealing. Has it struck you that you yourself have been stealing in some of these ways? If so, God calls you now to repent (which means, change) and make restitution to those you have defrauded. Zacchaeus, the artist in extortion, expressed his repentance by promising to restore fourfold all the money he had taken unjustly (Luke 19:8; Zacchaeus was applying the four-sheep-for-one rule of Exodus 22:1). In the Belfast revival of 1922-23, converted shipyard workers brought back tools and equipment which they had "knocked off" in such quantities that in one place an additional store shed had to be provided to hold them. That showed spiritual reality. How much reality of this kind is there about us?

Further Bible Study

Thieving and cheating in the family:
• Genesis 27; 29:15-30; 30:25-31:42

Questions for Thought and Discussion

- Why do you think Luther saw taking advantage of others as a form of theft?
- How is stealing related to the exhortation, "owe no man anything"?
- Do you agree that a man's reputation is more important than his wallet? Why or why not?

13

Truth Is Sacred

If I call you a liar, you will feel deeply insulted, for we think of liars, persons whose word we cannot trust, as morally pretty far gone. From the ninth commandment, and much else in the Bible, we learn that this is God's estimate too. Some treat lying as a kind of fine art, but Scripture views it with horror, and our Anglo-Saxon conviction about the sanctity of truth and the shamefulness of lying reflects the Bible's health-giving influence on our culture.

False Witness

The command not to "bear false witness against your neighbor" comes in Exodus 20:16 and Deuteronomy 5:20. The word for "false" in the first text means "untrue," that in the second means "insincere," thus pointing to the deceitful purpose which breeds the falsehood. The NEB rendering, "give false evidence," highlights the fact that the commandment relates in the first place to the law-court, where justice can only be done if witnesses tell "the truth, the whole truth, and nothing but the truth"—a formula which forcibly reminds us that exaggerations, half-truths, and misleading silences can all in effect be lies. But the principle of holding truth sacred goes beyond the law-court, and touches all our living.

Why Lie?

Why do people lie to and about each other? Why, for that matter, did Satan ("a liar and the father of lies" according to our Lord in John 8:44) lie to Eve in the garden? Partly from malice, partly from pride. When you lie to do someone down, it is malice; when you lie to impress, move, and use him, and to keep him from seeing you in a bad light, it is pride. Satan lied (and lies) because he hates God and godly folk, and wants to extend his anti-God revolt. Men lie to shield themselves from exposure and to further their supposed interests. Wounded Jewish pride spawned false witness in court against both Jesus and Stephen (Matthew 26:59ff.; Acts 6:13). Fear, contempt, and revenge, boastful conceit, fraud, and the desire to shine by telling a good story are other motives which prompt lies.

Indeed, lying in some shape or form (including "white lies," which are rarely as white as we make out) is so universal an activity as to constitute compelling proof of our fallenness, just as do the locks on all our home and car doors.

God and Lies

Lying insults not only your neighbor, whom you may manage to fool, but also God, whom you can never fool. A truth-telling, promise-keeping God who "cannot lie" (Titus 1:2, NEB; also Numbers 23:19; 1 Samuel 15:29), and who wants to see in us his own moral image, naturally "hates . . . a lying tongue . . . a false witness who breathes out lies" (Proverbs 6:16-19). Lying is part of Satan's image, not God's, and we should not wonder that "every one who loves and practices falsehood" should thereby exclude himself from God's city (Revelation 22:15; cf. 21:27). There is no godliness without truthfulness. Lord, have mercy!

Truth and Love

But when one sets out to be truthful, new problems appear. There are people to whom it is clearly not right to tell the whole truth—invalids, not yet strong enough to take bad news; enemies in wartime, to whom one should not give information, and from whom, like Rahab (Joshua 2) and Corrie ten Boom, one may have fugitives to hide; mad and bad folk, who would use what you tell them to harm others; the general public, when as a politician one is putting through a beneficent plan which depends for its effect on nobody anticipating it; and so on. Nobody doubts that in these cases responsible persons must dissemble. But does that square with the ninth commandment?

In principle, yes. What is forbidden is false witness against your neighbor—that is, as we said, prideful lying designed to do him down, and exalt you at his expense. The positive command implicit in this negative is that we should seek our neighbor's good, and speak truth to him and about him to this end. When the love which seeks his good prompts us to withhold truth which, if spoken, would bring him harm, the spirit of the ninth commandment is being observed. In such exceptional cases as we have mentioned, all courses of action have something of evil in them, and an outright lie, like that of Rahab (Joshua 2:4, 5; note the commendation of her, James 2:25) may actually be the best way, the least evil, and the truest expression of love to all the parties involved.

Yet a lie, even when prompted by love, loyalty, and an escapable recognition that if telling it is bad, not telling it would be worse, remains an evil thing (unless, indeed, with old-style Jesuits and modern-type situationists we hold that the end justifies the means). To bear false witness for one's neighbor is not so bad as bearing false witness against him; but the lie as such, however necessary it appears, is bad, not good, and the right-minded man knows this. Rightly will he feel defiled; rightly will he seek fresh cleansing in the blood of Christ, and settle for living the only way anyone can live with our holy God—by the forgiveness of sins. Again, we say: Lord, have mercy!—and lead us not into this particular type of temptation, where only a choice of sins seems open to us, but deliver us from evil.

Further Bible Study

False witness:
- 1 Kings 21:1-24
- Acts 6:8-15
- Matthew 26:57-75

Questions for Thought and Discussion

- Why is truthfulness important not only in the courtroom, but in all life?
- Why did Satan lie to Eve? Do you ever misrepresent the truth with the same motives?
- Why can there be no godliness without truthfulness?

14

Be Content

In the tenth commandment, "you shall not covet," God's searchlight moves from actions to attitudes, from motions to motives, from forbidden deeds to forbidden desire. The word for "covet" conveys the thought of seeking dishonest and dishonorable gain. Coveting appears here as first cousin to envy: you see what someone else has, and you want to grab it for yourself, as Ahab wanted to grab Naboth's vineyard in 1 Kings 21. In Colossians 3:5, Paul calls coveting idolatry, because the things coveted become your god, controlling your life.

Coveting is a root of all social evil; desires that burst the bounds beget actions to match. David took Bathsheba (thus, by theft, breaking the eighth commandment) and got her pregnant (thus breaking the seventh) and then to avoid scandal arranged for her husband Uriah to be killed (thus breaking the sixth), and it all began with David coveting his neighbor's wife, in breach of the tenth (see 2 Samuel 11).

Similarly, Ahab's coveting of Naboth's vineyard next door led to the framing of Naboth by false witness (breaking the ninth commandment), his judicial murder (breaking the sixth), and his vineyard being forfeited to the crown—in other words, legally stolen (breaking the eighth).

Then there was Achan (Joshua 7; note verse 21), and also Judas, whose coveting led him to break first the eighth commandment (John 12:6) and then the sixth and ninth together as he betrayed Jesus to death by a simulated act of homage (Matthew 26:48-50), all for money (Matthew 26:14-16; cf. 27:3-5). Perhaps Paul had Achan and Judas in mind, as well as folk known to him directly, when he wrote that "the love of money is the root of all evils; it is through this craving that some have wandered away from the faith and pierced their hearts with many pangs" (1 Timothy 6:10).

Called to Contentment

Put positively, "you shall not covet . . . anything that is your neighbor's" is a call to contentment with one's lot. The contentment which the tenth commandment prescribes is the supreme safeguard against temptations to break commandments five to nine. The discontented man, whose inner itch makes him self-absorbed, sees other people as tools to use in order to feed his greed, but the contented man is free as others are not to concentrate on treating his neighbor right. "There is great gain in godliness with contentment," wrote Paul (1 Timothy 6:6).

Scripture presents contentment as a spiritual secret. It is one dimension of happiness, which is itself the fruit of a relationship. Toplady focuses this superbly in a poem beginning "Happiness, thou lovely name, Where's thy seat, O tell me, where?" He writes:

> *Object of my first desire,*
> *Jesus, crucified for me!*
> *All to happiness aspire,*
> *Only to be found in thee.*
> *Thee to please and thee to know*
> *Constitute our bliss below,*
> *Thee to see and thee to love*
> *Constitute our bliss above.*
>
>
> *Whilst I feel thy love to me,*
> *Every object teems with joy;*
> *Here, O may I walk with thee,*
> *Then into thy presence die!*

Let me but thyself possess,
Total sum of happiness!
Real bliss I then shall prove,
Heaven below, and heaven above.

Knowing the love of Christ is the one and only source from which true contentment ever flows.

Jesus diagnosed, however, one mortal enemy to contentment: worry (see Matthew 6:25-34). But, he said, for a child of God (and every Christian is that) worry, which is in any case useless, since it can improve nothing (verse 27), is quite unnecessary. Why? Because "your heavenly Father knows" your needs (verse 32) and can be relied on to supply them as you "seek first his kingdom and his righteousness" (verse 33). Not to see this, and to lose one's contentment in consequence, shows "little faith" (verse 30). The God whose fatherhood is perfect can be trusted absolutely to care for us on a day-to-day basis. So to realize that while planning is a duty and worry is a sin, because God is in charge, and to face all circumstances with an attitude of "praise God, anyway" is a second secret of the contented life.

Nor is this all. Look at Paul, a contented man if ever there was one. From prison he wrote, "Not that I complain of want; for I have learned, in whatever state I am, to be content . . . I have learned the secret of facing . . . abundance and want. I can do all things [i.e., all that I am called to do] in him who strengthens me" (Philippians 4:11-13). The open secret to which Paul alludes here is fully spelled out in Hebrews 13:5ff.—"Put greed out of your lives and be content with whatever you have; God himself has said: *I will not fail you or desert you*, and so we can say with confidence: *With the Lord to help me, I fear nothing: what can man do to me?*" (JB). To realize the promised presence of one's loving Lord, who both orders one's circumstances and gives strength to cope with them, is the final secret of content.

Directing Desire

We are all, of course, creatures of desire; God made us so, and philosophies like Stoicism and religions like Buddhism which aim at the extinction of desire are really inhuman in their thrust. But desire that is sinfully disordered needs redirecting, so that we stop coveting others' goods and long instead for their good, and God's glory with and through it. When Thomas Chalmers spoke of "the expulsive power of a new affection," he was thinking of the way in which knowledge of my Savior's love diverts me from the barren ways of covetous self-service, to put God first, others second, and self-gratification last in my concerns. How much do we know in experience of this divine transforming power? It is here that the final antidote to covetousness is found.

Further Bible Study

From discontent to contentment:
• Psalm 73
Contentment in prison:
• Philippians 4:4-20

Questions for Thought and Discussion

• How is the contentment prescribed in the tenth commandment a safeguard against temptations to break the first nine?
• Do you agree that philosophies which aim at the extinction of desire are misguided? Why or why not?
• What did Thomas Chalmers mean by his phrase "the expulsive power of a new affection"?

15

Learning from
the Law

What does God want to teach us today from the Commandments? Some talk as if there is nothing for modern man to learn from them, but that is not so. Though more than 3,000 years old, this ancient piece of divine instruction is a revelation of God's mind and heart for all time, just as is the nearly-2,000-years-old gospel, and its relevance to us is at least threefold.

First, the Commandments show *what sort of people God wants us to be*. From the list of prohibitions, telling us what actions God hates, we learn the behavior he wishes and loves to see. What does God in the law say "No!" to? Unfaithfulness and irreverence to himself, and dishonor and damage to our neighbor. And who is our neighbor? Jesus, asked that question, replied in effect: everyone we meet. So what does God want us to be? Persons free of these evils; persons who actively love the God who made them and their neighbors, whom he also made, every day of their lives; persons, in fact, just like Jesus, who was not only God's eternal Son but also his perfect man. A tall order? Yes, but it should not cause surprise that our holy Creator requires us to reflect his moral glory. What else could possibly please him?

Three Uses

Rightly, Reformation theology did not separate God's law from God himself, but thought of it personally and dynamically, as a word which God is continually publishing to the world through Scripture and conscience, and through which he works constantly in human lives. Spelling out this approach, Reformed theologians said that God's law has three uses, or functions: first, to maintain order in society; second, to convince us of sin and drive us to Christ for life; third, to spur us on in obedience, by means of its standards and its sanctions, all of which express God's own nature. It is the third use that is in view here.

The Law of Nature

Second, the Commandments show *what sort of life-style is truly natural for us.* Rightly have theologians understood the Commandments as declaring "natural" law, the law of our nature. This phrase means that what is commanded not only corresponds to (though going beyond) "the work of the law" written, more or less fully, on every man's conscience (see Romans 2:12ff.), but also outlines the only form of conduct that fully satisfies human nature. Deviations from it, even where unconscious, are inescapably unfulfilling. When people shy away from the formula "God first, others second, self last," as if it were a recipe for total misery, they show that they do not understand themselves. Actually, this is the only formula that has ever brought true inward freedom and contentment on a life-long basis to anyone, and we should be glad that Christ our Master leads his disciples so firmly back to it.

People ask whether God's law binds all men or only believers. The answer is that it binds all—first, because God made us all; and second, because we are so made that without learning to obey the law we can never find the happiness and fulfillment we were made for.

There is a paradox here, which it is best not to conceal but to parade. The fulfillment of which we speak here is known only from the inside, by those who taste and see; from the outside it regularly looks to us like its exact opposite. This reflects Satan's success in persuading us, as once he persuaded Eve, that there is no fulfillment without unrestricted self-indulgence—one of the many optical illusions of the mind which he has spawned. But Jesus spoke parabolically of destroying one's own hand, foot, or eye in order to enter into life (Mark 9:43-48), and literally of forgoing marriage for the kingdom's sake (Matthew 19:12), and called all his followers to deny themselves; i.e., to be ready at his word to say "no" to anything and everything to which it would be most natural to say "yes." Can this be fulfillment? Yes—because God uses our willed detachment to attach us to himself, and fill us with himself, and that means life, light, and joy within. Christians jump into what felt to the probing toe like bitterly cold water, and find it lovely. But the world cannot discern the optical illusion, and remains skeptical.

Know Yourself

Third, the Commandments show *what sort of people we are in God's eyes*—namely, lawbreakers under sentence, whose only hope lies in God's forgiving mercy. When we measure our lives by God's law, we find that self-justification and self-satisfaction are alike impossible, and we are plunged into self-despair. The producing of this effect is what the Reformers called the second use of the law. In Romans 7:7-20, Paul tells us from his own experience how it works. The law trains a searchlight on our motives and desires (Paul instances coveting), and makes us aware in ourselves of a lawless energy—you could almost call it an instinctual drive—causing forbidden motives and desires to keep bubbling up, "making me captive to the law of sin which dwells in my members" (verse 23). Thus the law, by exposing us to ourselves as spiritually sick and lost, enables us to appreciate the gospel remedy.

> *Let us love, and sing, and wonder;*
> *Let us praise the Saviour's name!*
> *He has hushed the law's loud thunder,*
> *He has quenched Mount Sinai's flame;*
> *He has washed us with his blood,*
> *He presents our souls to God!*

Hallelujah!

Further Bible Study

How the law exposes sin:
- Romans 3:9-20; 7:7-25

How the law spurs the saint:
- Psalm 119

Questions for Thought and Discussion

- How do you explain the abiding relevance of the Commandments?
- What is meant by saying that the Commandments declare "the law of our nature"?
- What do the Commandments tell you about yourself? What have you done about it, and what do you intend to do about it now?

16

The Cement of Society

So far, we have treated the Commandments as God's address
to the individual ("you"), whereby he isolates us from the
crowd in which our identity would otherwise be sunk and
requires of us responsible personal reaction to what he says. This is
a true view of them, but it is not the whole truth. For the "you"
whom God first addressed in Exodus 20 and Deuteronomy 5 was
Israel corporately, the nation-family which he had redeemed ("I am
the LORD your God, who brought you out . . . "). And what God
was teaching was his will not only for individual Israelites, but also
for Israel's community life.

This too is truth for us, because it is truth for humanity as such.
God made us to live in societies—family, church, body politic, the
communities of business and culture—and the Commandments
show God's social ideal, as well as his purpose for individuals.
Indeed, the furthering of good order in society was for the
Reformers, as we noted earlier, the first use of the law.

The Way of Stability

What is God's ideal? A God-fearing community, marked by common worship (1, 2, 3) and an accepted rhythm of work and rest (4),
plus an unqualified respect for marriage and the family (5, 7), for
property and owner's rights (8, 10), for human life and each man's

claim on our protection (6), and for truth and honesty in all relationships (9).

God's concern for communities must not be thought of as second to his concern for individuals (the way our own concern so often shapes up), for in him the two concerns are organically one. This is clear from the way in which the Old Testament repeatedly sums up his promise, which was Israel's hope, in one treasure-chest word, *shalom*. *Shalom*, translated "peace," proves when unpacked to mean, not just freedom from war and trouble, sin and irreligion, but also justice, prosperity, good fellowship, and health, and all-round communal well-being under God's gracious hand.

Modern Western Christians, who have been conditioned by their culture to wear the blinkers of a rationalistic individualism, and who are constantly being deafened by the clamor of humanists, for whom society's whole purpose is to extend the individual's range of choices, may find the unity of God's concern for the-individual-in-community and the-community-of-individuals hard to see. But that is our problem. Other generations could see it, and in Scripture the matter is clear.

So God's Commandments are in truth cement for society. It is clear that where these values are acknowledged, communities (our own, for instance, in the past) hold together, even in this fallen world; but in proportion as these values are negated, society falls apart. This can be learned both from the paganized world of injustice and revolution which was the northern kingdom of Israel (trace its sad story in 1 Kings 12-2 Kings 17, and the prophecies of Amos and Hosea), and also from the revolutions and counterrevolutions that rack the world today.

The Secular State

Till recently most Western nations saw themselves as a continuation of medieval Christendom—that is, as social and political entities with corporate Christian commitments and ideals for living which, at least in intention, were controlled and shaped by Scripture. But now this ideal is being displaced by that of the secular state—a community that is officially without any religion or ideology save that of maximizing freedom for citizens to pursue as individuals whatever interests, religious or otherwise, they happen to have.

The change is gradual, and so the issue it raises is to some extent masked; but it is important to get it clear. Christian civilization, with its concern for the individual's health, welfare, and dignity, for integrity in public administration, and for a family life in which womanhood is honored and children's claims acknowledged, is a distinctively Christian product. Western society today is busily secularizing these concerns—that is, detaching them from their historic rootage in Christian faith, and dismissing that faith as no longer a viable basis for community life. For the moment, Western society seems so caring and compassionate that some view the secular city of today as the modern form of the kingdom of God. But, true as it is that through God's common grace good moral insights are regularly found among fallen men, Christian standards and values cannot last in a society that has corporately apostatized from Christian faith.

Judgment

Why is this? Not only because denying the absolutes of faith undercuts moral absolutes too (though indeed it does), but also because moral corruption and the misery it brings are part of God's judgment on apostasy. "Since they did not see fit to acknowledge God, God gave them up to a base mind and to improper conduct," says Paul, and continues with a sample catalog of horrors that reads like a summary of the news in this morning's paper (Romans 1:28-31). Our much-vaunted "permissiveness" is actually a matter of divine curse, as was the idiotically cheerful lawlessness of Jeremiah's day. What thoughtful person can look ahead without a shudder?

What then should we say of the modern secular society? Should we see its emergence as a sign of progress? Is it not rather a sign of decadence, the start of a slide down a slippery slope with a pit at the bottom? When God's values are ignored, and the only community ideal is permissiveness, where will moral capital come from once the Christian legacy is spent? How can national policy ever rise above material self-interest, pragmatic and unprincipled? How can internal collapse be avoided as sectional interests, unrestrained by any sense of national responsibility, cut each other down? How can an overall reduction, indeed destruction, of happiness be avoided, when the revealed way of happiness, the "God first, others next, self last" of the Commandments, is rejected? The prospects are ominous. May God bring us back to himself, and to the social wisdom of his Commandments before it is too late.

Further Bible Study

Dynamics of the permissive society:
- Romans 1:18-32

Analysis of the apostate society:
- Isaiah 1, 3, 5

Questions for Thought and Discussion

- Do you agree that the Commandments are meant for societies as well as individuals? Why or why not?
- Does a society's attitude to the Commandments affect its future? In what way?
- What replaces the Commandments in the secular state? With what result?

Index